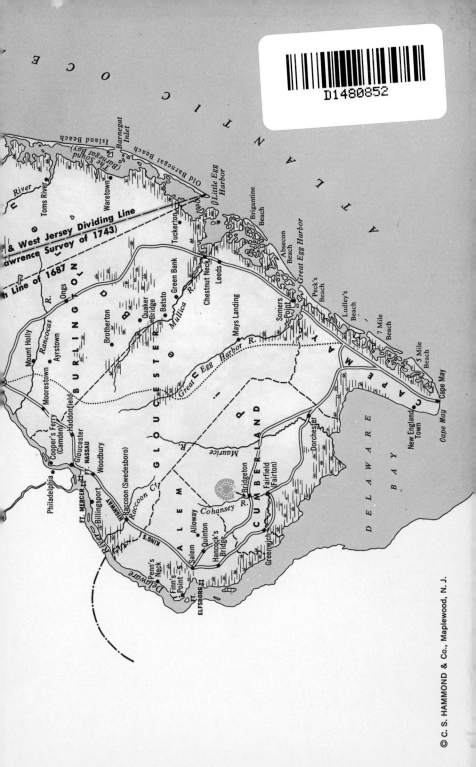

ATLANTIC OCEAN

River
Toms River
Waretown
Barnegat Beach
Island Beach
The Sound (Barnegat Bay)
Old Barnegat Beach
Barnegat Inlet

& West Jersey Dividing Line
awrence Survey of 1743)
h Line of 1687

BURLINGTON

Tuckerton
Little Egg Harbor
Brigantine Beach

Ongs
R.
Green Bank
Batsto
Quaker Bridge
Chestnut Neck
Leeds
Absecon Beach
Great Egg Harbor
Somers Point
Peck's Beach

Mount Holly
Rancocas R.
Ayrstown
Brotherton
Mullica R.
Mays Landing
Great Egg Harbor R.
Ludley's Beach
7 Mile Beach
5 Mile Beach

Moorestown
GLOUCESTER
Dorchester
Cape May
New England Town
Cape May

Cooper's Ferry (Camden)
Haddonfield
Gloucester
FT. NASSAU
Woodbury
Raccoon (Swedesboro)
Maurice R.
CUMBERLAND
DELAWARE BAY

Philadelphia
FT. MERCER
Billingsport
SALEM
KING'S
Alloway
Quinton
Cohansey
Bridgeton
Fairfield (Fairton)
Greenwich
DELAWARE

Penn's Neck
Finn's Point
FT. ELFSBORG
Salem
Hancock's Bridge

*New Jersey and the
English Colonization of
North America*

THE NEW JERSEY HISTORICAL SERIES

Edited by

RICHARD M. HUBER   WHEATON J. LANE

Other books in the series will be announced

Volume 3

The New Jersey Historical Series

New Jersey and the
English Colonization of
North America

WESLEY FRANK CRAVEN

1964

D. VAN NOSTRAND COMPANY, INC.

Princeton, New Jersey

New York, N. Y. · *Toronto, Canada* · *London, England*

D. VAN NOSTRAND COMPANY, INC.
120 Alexander St., Princeton, New Jersey (*Principal office*)
24 West 40 Street, New York 18, New York

D. VAN NOSTRAND COMPANY, LTD.
358, Kensington High Street, London, W.14, England

D. VAN NOSTRAND COMPANY (*Canada*), LTD.
25 Hollinger Road, Toronto 16, Canada

Published simultaneously in Canada by
D. VAN NOSTRAND COMPANY (Canada), LTD.

FOREWORD

Many tracks will be left by the New Jersey Tercentenary celebration, but few will be larger than those made by the New Jersey Historical Series. The Series is a monumental publishing project—the product of a remarkable collaborative effort between public and private enterprise.

New Jersey has needed a series of books about itself. The 300th anniversary of the State is a fitting time to publish such a series. It is to the credit of the State's Tercentenary Commission that this series has been created.

In an enterprise of such scope, there must be many contributors. Each of these must give considerably of himself if the enterprise is to succeed. The New Jersey Historical Series, the most ambitious publishing venture ever undertaken about a state, was conceived by a committee of Jerseymen—Julian F. Boyd, Wesley Frank Craven, John T. Cunningham, David S. Davies, and Richard P. McCormick. Not only did these men outline the need for such an historic venture; they also aided in the selection of the editors of the series.

Both jobs were well done. The volumes speak for themselves. The devoted and scholarly services of

Richard M. Huber and Wheaton J. Lane, the editors, are a part of every book in the series. The editors have been aided in their work by two fine assistants, Elizabeth Jackson Holland and Bertha DeGraw Miller.

To D. Van Nostrand Company, Inc. my special thanks for recognizing New Jersey's need and for bringing their skills and publishing wisdom to bear upon the printing and distributing of the New Jersey Historical Series.

RICHARD J. HUGHES
Governor of the
State of New Jersey

January, 1964

PREFACE

New Jersey's early history is not an easy story to tell. Some of the difficulty comes from the inescapable complexity belonging to certain parts of the story. Some of it is attributable to the state of the record, which at critical points is remarkably incomplete and at other points badly tangled. Still another source of the difficulty, and possibly the most serious, is the exceptional dependence of New Jersey's history upon developments outside the colony's own limits.

Thus, at the very beginning, there is no way of getting into New Jersey's history without first taking account of the English conquest of New Amsterdam. Had that venture failed, the deed of lease and release by which James, Duke of York, conferred title to the fertile acres and rolling hills lying between the Hudson and the Delaware upon John Lord Berkeley and Sir George Carteret on June 24, 1664—the document from which the State dates its current Tercentenary celebrations —would have remained an item of little more than antiquarian interest for students of American history. In short, there would have been no New Jersey.

It is no great exaggeration to say that the conquest of New Amsterdam merely brought to completion a task initially undertaken by the New England Puritans. For many years past they had been busily engaged in cutting down Dutch New Netherland to a size more appropriate to their own ambitions, and they were prompt in following up the conquest by settlement on the Jersey side of the Hudson. Except for a small group of Dutch farmers planted at Bergen as late as 1660, New Jersey was first developed as a further projection of Puritan New England. After the Puritans, there came from England the Quakers who began an especially significant social experiment on the Jersey bank of the Delaware, but soon transferred their headquarters across the river to a newly established Philadelphia. Colonial New Jersey, it must be understood, was not so much a single community as, rather, a province comprising two separate and distinct communities, each of them belonging to a larger community which found the center of its life outside the province. In other words, the colony was very much like the modern State, with half its population oriented toward Philadelphia and half toward New York and New England.

New Jersey's history must be read, first of all, as an integral part of the larger story of the middle colonies—those which in the second half of the seventeenth century provided a link between the earlier English settlements on the Chesapeake and in New England and so gave shape to our common history. Nor is it enough to keep an eye upon the development of New Jersey's immediate neighbors. Not even Carolina or the West Indies can be excluded from the story. Indeed, the most important single document in New Jersey's early history, the Concessions and Agreement of 1665, was initially drafted by the Carolina proprietors, who included both New Jersey proprietors in their number. This charter, in which men were given to understand their rights as they took up land in the colony, was issued for the assurance of Barbadian planters who hoped to find their fortunes in Carolina. There were even a few Barbadians who followed its generous guarantees all the way up from the West Indies to New Jersey.

Perhaps we can better understand New Jersey's beginnings simply by trying to tell the story in full context. If by taking this approach it becomes necessary to slight some familiar detail, it is possible that a new appreciation of the story's salient features may be gained. Perhaps, too, we can thereby bring into better perspective the later phase of England's colonizing activity in North America, a subject which for too long has been studied piecemeal in response to special parochial and provincial interests. It is one of the more important chapters of American history, and New Jersey's part in it is of no small significance.

Happily, another volume in the Tercentenary Series, *New Jersey from Colony to State*, presents a detailed account of New Jersey's colonial experience within the framework of the State's own history. Men and events omitted here receive the attention due them in that and other volumes of the Series. What follows is basically an interpretive essay intended primarily to place New Jersey's story in the broad setting of England's developing interest in North America.

WESLEY FRANK CRAVEN

Princeton, New Jersey
January, 1964

x

TABLE OF CONTENTS

LIST OF ILLUSTRATIONS

The Stony Brook Meeting House of the Society of Friends at Princeton, 1726. *Photograph by Alan W. Richards*

I

THE RESTORATION COLONIES

England acquired most of the colonies destined to give dominance on the North American continent to an English-speaking people in two main, and somewhat discrete, periods of activity. From the small and tragically difficult beginning at Jamestown in 1607, the movement of colonists across the Atlantic broadened out, both numerically and geographically, until it reached full tide during the decade of the 1630's. Virginia was followed by Lord Baltimore's colony of Maryland and by the Puritan occupation of New England. Simultaneously, thousands of Englishmen migrated to the Lesser Antilles of the West Indies. Then came in the 1640's the English Civil War from which the Puritans emerged triumphant and, after the execution of King Charles I in 1649, the Puritan Interregnum over which Oliver Cromwell presided. All told, the homeland experienced two decades of political instability that produced a distinct break in England's colonizing activity. Except for Cromwell's conquest of Jamaica in 1655, no new colonies were acquired by England until after the Restoration of 1660.

This political settlement owed its designation to the re-establishment in that year of the monarchy. The reign of the restored King Charles II, extending from 1660 to his death in 1685, witnessed a decided revival of interest in the extension of English posessions in North America. No less than six of the 13 original states of our Federal Union were first occupied by Englishmen during the Restoration era: New York, New Jersey, Pennsylvania, Delaware, and the two Carolinas. After the settlement of Pennsylvania in 1682, moreover, only Georgia remained to be founded, and that event came closer, in point of time, to the American Revolution than it did to the settlement of Pennsylvania. New Jersey's story falls thus into the second, and very nearly the final, phase of a colonizing effort that traditionally, and quite properly, has been viewed as the beginning of the history of the United States.

Several considerations serve to mark this Restoration phase of England's colonial expansion as a continuation of the first phase, and no other more so than the fact that the initiative now was taken very largely by colonists who had reached America somewhat earlier in the century. But to make this point of continuity is also to state a point of sharp contrast between the two periods. The settlements in Virginia, Maryland, New England, and the West Indies had been accomplished by a direct migration of colonists from England, in a movement of population depending at first upon heavy subsidies from promoters who remained resident in England. On the other hand, among the great men who promoted settlements during the Restoration era, only William Penn, as the leader of Quaker colonization in the Delaware Valley, sponsored a significant migration from the British Isles.* All the others, including New Jersey's original proprietors, were content to base their plans upon the prospect of enlisting their settlers from communities already established in America. More than that, most of these men seem to have been prompted to lend the prestige of their names to new colonizing ventures by proposals coming to them from America.

In this kind of. adventure one finds nothing heroic, nothing that is comparable to the dedicated services rendered, for example, to the colony of Virginia in its earliest years by Sir Thomas Smith or by Sir Edwin Sandys. Fewer judgments of history have been more soundly based than that which has awarded high honors among the later promoters of English colonization in North America to William Penn alone. Another exception possibly should be made for the Earl of Shaftesbury, who became the leading spirit among the Carolina proprietors. In fact, he probably

* This difference, no doubt, owed something to the changing attitude in England toward emigration into the colonies. Through the first half of the century, public policy had been generally favorable, but the trend of opinion after the Restoration was toward the view that such a migration represented a loss of strength to the nation.

saved the Carolina venture from complete collapse by persuading most of the proprietors, though by no means all, in 1669 to put a little money into their common undertaking, something they theretofore had neglected to do. But it should be noted that Shaftesbury proposed to spend the fund, or most of it at any rate, on assistance to residents of the West Indian island of Barbados who previously had been left to carry virtually the whole burden of the Carolina venture alone. John Lord Berkeley and Sir George Carteret were fully representative of Restoration promoters, and in no way more so than in the limited investment they were willing to make for the development of their joint proprietorship in New Jersey.

This observation is not intended as one of disparagement. The policies pursued by the Restoration proprietors were, for the most part, shrewdly conceived. They were policies, moreover, which gave recognition to principles of great importance for the history of our country. Especially significant were the guarantees of religious and political rights offered as inducements for settlement in the new colonies. As public-spirited as they were self-seeking, the proprietors earnestly sought to advance the interests of England, and in this purpose they achieved much. If they seem to have left too much of the work to be done by colonists already living in America, it is also true that these colonists might not have accomplished all that they did without the support, other than financial, they received from the great men in London.

Before turning to the London side of the story, it will be helpful to look more closely at the situation in America which the Restoration promoters undertook to turn to their own and to England's advantage.

Our attention is claimed, above all, by a type of folk migration (perhaps imperialism would not be too strong a word to use) that must be given first place in any attempt to explain an extraordinary expansion of the areas originally occupied by the English colonists. This folk migration, folk wandering, or folk imperialism, whatever may be the preferred term, was destined to exert an especially important influence on the subsequent course of American history. The subject is usually discussed in the context of later settlements on the trans-Appalachian frontier, as though it represents a relatively late development in our history. In the occupations of Tennessee, of Kentucky, or of Oregon, to mention but three, we have pridefully followed the achievements of men who depended very largely upon their own resources, and who found their leadership among the people who intended themselves to occupy the new territory. We have seen them as men who welcomed the assistance of government, who preferred in fact to move with the sanctions government alone could give, but who did not hesitate to seize the initiative that might prompt the government to act in their behalf. We have found cause to assume, in some instances, that they were men who might have brought their ventures to full success without any aid from government, except such a government as may have been created by their own resourcefulness. We have boasted that they were a peculiar breed of men: men bred by the American frontier, by the inviting opportunities of the North American continent. In this we have not been wholly wrong, but all too often of late we have tended to forget that this breed of men made a very early appearance in American history—early enough, indeed, to have given shape to the history of New Jersey.

However one may wish to describe this feature of American history, it had deep roots in the experience of the original seaboard colonies. In fact, its deepest roots must be sought in the developing pattern of England's colonization of the New World during the early years of the seventeenth century.

From the very first efforts by Sir Humphrey Gilbert and Sir Walter Raleigh, the English government had shown no inclination to take the initiative. Instead, it limited its own role to the issuance of royal charters lending sanction to ventures by individuals or groups of individuals joined together for the achievement of their own ends. The initiative might be taken by a joint-stock corporation modeled after the great companies engaged in extending England's trade into Muscovy, the Levant, and India—as in the case of the Virginia Company or the Massachusetts Bay Company. The initiative might be seized by a religious group, persuaded not only that its project was undertaken in the interest of England but that its work was the work of the Lord. Here the classic example is found, of course, in the Puritan settlement of New England. Or, the initiative might be that of such an individual as Lord Baltimore, who had acquired extensive properties in England and Ireland and entertained the hope of a much greater expansion of his personal estate in America. Whatever the case, public policy encouraged the king's subjects to fix and pursue their own objectives, and this they did in great variety.

The initial settlement in Virginia owed its success to the expenditure of vast funds subscribed in London. Shortly, however, the returns on this investment proved to be so meager, in comparison with the high hopes which had inspired it, that it became impossible for the Virginia Company to float additional subscriptions. The project was kept alive after 1616 by the discovery that colonization could become very largely a self-supporting enterprise simply by promising that a specified acreage, soon commonly known as the headright, would be deeded to anyone who paid the way of a colonist to Virginia, including the man who paid his own way. This headright has become identified in our histories chiefly with the institution of indentured servitude, under which even the humblest of Englishmen might get to America at his own charge by agreeing to work out the cost of his passage in the colony. But the headright has a much greater significance than that familiar practice at first glance suggests. The principle it represents—the use of undeveloped land in America to subsidize the immigration needed for its development—is the principle upon which all of the English colonizers, in one way or another, thereafter depended for financing an obviously expensive movement of population across the Atlantic. To put the point briefly, not only had English promoters discovered at an early date how to make their undertaking nearly self-supporting, but there were few Englishmen living here at the middle of the seventeenth century who could not claim, as did Thomas Jefferson on the eve of the Revolution, that they had paid their own way to America.

In America they had found what our earliest historians were fond of describing as a wilderness, and by their own labor they had begun the work of converting that wilderness into the garden of which later generations would proudly boast. Confident as to who it was who had carried the main burden in opening America to English enterprise, these colonists showed no reluctance to take the lead in further efforts to extend the area of their occupancy. For all the heavy labor that is required in clearing new ground, and the hope the first settlers undoubtedly had of reproducing here the more desirable features of life in England, these were remarkably "footloose" men, quick to move the site of their endeavors to some new and presumably more inviting location. And as they moved, whether as individuals or as communities, as often was the case in New England, they showed themselves to be remarkably self-sufficient men.

In New England the Puritans had begun their settlement within the narrow bounds fixed by the charter of the Massachusetts Bay Company. But soon these Puritans, stimulated only in small part by their religious differences, were spilling over into New Hampshire and the lower reaches of Maine, into Rhode Island, and into Connecticut, whence by the 1640's they were moving across the great sound in increasing numbers onto Long Island. Unable at first to claim the assistance of a friendly government at home, and subsequently left largely to their own devices by the triumphant Puritans in England, the New England colonizers moved out from Massachusetts Bay in full confidence of divine approval. Were they not God's elect, His own chosen people, men who had dared to cross the Atlantic and accept the dangers of life in the wilderness in order that His will might prevail among mankind? Such, certainly, was their assumption. Wherever they went the town meeting, drawing its usages from the congregational pattern of church polity and the ancient custom of the English parish, provided the rudimentary elements of an effective civil authority. Moreover, when necessary, the towns showed a marked capacity for joining together to form larger jurisdictions, as in the cases of those centered in Rhode Island, New Haven, and the Connecticut River Valley. The process was even carried another step forward in 1643 by the organization of the New England Confederation, a union of several distinct jurisdictions that had no parallel in our history until the formation of the National union at the time of the Revolution.

By 1650 Peter Stuyvesant, director-general for the Dutch West India Company at New Amsterdam, knew that New England's restless expansion was a challenge to the very existence of thinly-populated New Netherland. Lacking the force that was needed to counter New England's vigorous thrust, he undertook by negotiation to fix a line that might limit the ambitions of his Puritan neighbors. According to the so-called Treaty of Hartford in 1650, the boundary between the English and Dutch jurisdictions would run, roughly north and south, through Oyster Bay on Long Island. The agreement was never ratified by Oliver Cromwell, who himself was at war with Holland from 1652 to 1654, and had that war lasted only a little longer, it is quite conceivable that New Netherland might have fallen to the New England Puritans almost ten years before its surrender to Richard Nicolls in 1664. As it turned out, if a complex story may be reduced to its simplest terms, the Puritans by 1664, were for all practical purposes in full control of Long Island and on the Connecticut shore they had extended their settlements as far west as Westchester. From Long Island, of course, it was only a jump across the bay to the Jersey shore, upon which more than one Puritan already had cast an appreciative eye.

In fact, the New Haven Puritans had established a trading settlement on the Jersey bank of the Delaware as early as 1641. At Varkens Kill (Salem Creek) they planted a community of 20 families, some of whom remained until 1643, when the project came to an end because it had failed to achieve its main purpose, which was a profitable trade with the Indians. An abortive attempt to reestablish the settlement followed in 1651, with great loss to the investors. Many of the New Haven Puritans were destined finally to find a home in New Jersey, but in quite a different part and for different reasons from those which had prompted these first ventures.

Meanwhile, other Englishmen had shown an active interest in the area, notably Sir Edmund Plowden, a Catholic gentleman who in 1634 secured a very generous grant of lands he described as New Albion. Embracing Long Island, the whole of what was to be New Jersey, and more besides, New Albion would have been a most impressive estate had its proprietor managed to bring the project into the realm of reality. From 1642 to 1648 Sir Edmund was resident in Virginia,

From Cotton Mather, *Magnalia Christi Americana: or, the Ecclesiastical History of New-England*, London, 1702

whence he dispatched men and ships to the Delaware, but nothing came of his efforts.

English adventurers had been interested in the Delaware Bay and River as early as 1609, when Captain Samuel Argall explored the coast above Virginia. The name itself perpetuates the memory of Lord De La Warr, Virginia's first governor. A little later, Lord Baltimore, in his Maryland Charter of 1632, had established a claim to title reaching all the way from Chesapeake Bay to the Delaware. But the Swedes and the Dutch had been left to accomplish the initial settlement of the Delaware Valley. Although the Dutch were the first to settle on what they called the South River, the Swedes held the upper hand there from 1638 until Stuyvesant conquered New Sweden in 1655. That conquest marked the high point in Stuyvesant's career, but it had been achieved at a cost the feeble Dutch West India Company was willing to meet only by the surrender of its rights on the Delaware to the City of Amsterdam. The settlers sent out by Amsterdam, perhaps as many as six hundred, to join the Swedes and Finns on the Delaware were to write, on the very eve of the English conquest of New Netherland, the most successful single chapter in the history of Dutch colonization in North America.

Even so, it would be difficult to exaggerate the weakness of New Netherland in 1664. Stuyvesant's own jurisdiction was now limited, for practical purposes, to the very thin line of settlement reaching up the Hudson from Manhattan to Fort Orange, or Albany as the English would soon know the place. Between the Hudson and the Delaware, in "New Jersey" as Englishmen were to call it, lay an area in which the native Indian remained virtually as free to pursue his ambitions as for generations past had been his ancestors. The handful of Dutch settlers at Bergen marked no more than a very short step toward settlement of the area. The more numerous population settled in the Delaware Valley lived, practically without exception, on the west bank of the river. A few of them now and again had crossed the river, perhaps to hunt or trade with the Indians, to expel some intruding Englishman, or to plant an occasional crop in obviously fertile soil, but most of the Swedes and the Dutch who settled in New Jersey did so after the English conquest. What is more immediately important is that the two main centers of settlement in Dutch New Netherland were widely separated, and hence unable to reinforce one another for purposes of defense.

The English settlements below the Delaware posed no such immediate threat to the Dutch position as did the Puritans of New England. But along the amazing system of inland waterways which join to form Chesapeake Bay, the English settlers were showing the same restless energy as their fellow countrymen to the north. By 1664 Lord Baltimore's colonists in Maryland were fast

From Richard Blome, *The Present State of His Majesties Isles and Territories in America*, London, 1687

drawing a full ring of settlement around the great bay, and only a relatively short distance separated them from the boundary Lord Baltimore claimed on the Delaware. In Maryland alone by 1664 there probably were more European settlers than in all New Netherland. Virginia, oldest and now decidedly the most populous of the English colonies in North America, having found its northward expansion checked at the Potomac by Baltimore's grant to Maryland, had turned its attention southward. The Virginians were taking up land on Albemarle Sound, in modern North Carolina, as early as 1660, perhaps even earlier.

A promise that the whole coastline reaching southward toward Spanish Florida would be claimed for English enterprise was the greater because of recent developments in Barbados. Oldest of the English West Indian plantations and, until the conquest of Jamaica in 1655, the largest, Barbados more than once before had served as the base for new colonizing ventures. Indeed, over the course of a quarter-century the West Indian planters, who first grew tobacco for their staple crop, had moved about from island to island of the Lesser Antilles in a bewildering pattern of settlement that almost defies description by the historian. There is nothing surprising in the interest that some of these planters showed at the time of the Restoration in a not-too-distant mainland on which their fellow countrymen were carving out empires far larger, if not more immediately remunerative, than any that could be built within the limited confines of the West Indies. Nor is there cause for surprise in the choice of Carolina. There Sir Walter Raleigh had first offered a challenge to Spain's pretentious claims in the New World, and the English West Indian colonists were fully entitled to view their own settlements as an especially significant development of that same challenge. Recently, moreover, the old spirit of rivalry with Spain had received fresh stimulation from Cromwell's Western Design, a grandly conceived scheme for seizure of all the Spanish West Indies. The project had failed in execution, except for the capture of Jamaica, but there can be no doubt that the attempt, in which William Penn's father commanded the English fleet, served to focus attention anew upon the strategically situated coast of Carolina.

Equally as important—and probably much more so—were the consequences of a basic change occurring at mid-century in the economy of the English West Indian plantations. Tobacco was giving place to sugar as the staple crop, and it was becoming clear that for the production of sugar there were distinct advantages in larger units of cultivation and the employment of Negro labor. The resulting consolidations of property progressively limited the prospects of many English settlers, and so caused them to look abroad for opportunities equal to the capital and labor they were willing to invest in a new adventure. In

as acceptable as possible by conforming with the prevailing urge toward a final restoration of political stability in the kingdom. Only in the settlement of religious issues did the Restoration government show a markedly vindictive spirit. Few men were executed, chiefly those who had been directly involved in the execution of Charles I, but the re-established Church of England came under the control of followers of the former archbishop William Laud who were determined to stamp out the last vestiges of Puritanism in England. They were, however, content to limit their efforts to England and showed no inclination whatever to extend their crusade into the colonies. Moreover, they displayed a remarkable indifference to appeals for assistance from fellow Anglicans in the colonies, as Sir William Berkeley soon discovered to his great sorrow. A generation would pass before the Anglican Church became fully alert to the great opportunity for missionary endeavor the American colonies so obviously offered. Meanwhile, the government found itself free to shape a colonial policy in which all questions of religion were subordinated to mundane considerations. From this turn of history came extraordinary contradictions in the policies of the Restoration government of Charles II. On the one hand, many Dissenters, mostly Quakers, were to be driven from England. On the other, many of them were to find a refuge, with the government's encouragement, in English America, where the Puritans of New England would receive favors denied the Anglican settlers of Virginia.

Among the considerations which gave shape to an emerging colonial policy, the chief was that of England's trade. The question had a special urgency at this time, partly because royal finances significantly depended upon the prosperity of that trade, and partly because of a continuing threat that the thrifty and shrewd merchants of Holland might drive their English competitors from the world's marketplaces, both old and new. Already Parliament had enacted the Navigation Act of 1660, which was destined to serve as the foundation of England's colonial policy for almost two centuries. This act established the strictest kind of monopolistic control over the trade of the West Indian and Chesapeake colonies, whose staples of sugar and tobacco could be useful in building England's prosperity, but it posed no more than a distant threat to the growing trade conducted by New England's enterprising merchants in the western Atlantic. Indeed, the Act contained provisions clearly intended for the encouragement of that trade, which was plied in competition with the Dutch and which in providing food for the West Indian plantations permitted a fuller conversion of the land there to sugar cane.

In further testimony that the Restoration government was disinclined to punish the Puritan colonies for their Puritanism, King Charles II offered in 1662 to confirm the Massachusetts charter with only such provisoes as were necessary to assure a proper acknowledgment of his own authority and the right of Anglicans to worship in their own way without prejudice. Puritan Massachusetts found the price too high, and persisted in a course of equivocation which soon cost it London's favor. But in that same year Connecticut, and in the next year Rhode Island, won royal charters conferring such full rights of self-government that these Puritan communities found no need to substitute different frames of government until long after the American Revolution.

Rhode Island's charter guaranteed complete religious freedom for all inhabitants of the province, and in phrases to which not even Roger Williams, stern advocate of the separation of church and state, could take exception. This famous provision is often cited in evidence of the sharp contrast between the restrictive religious policy of the Restoration government at home and the very liberal religious policy it pursued in the colonies. All too often overlooked, however, is the complete silence of the Connecticut charter on issues involving church and state. There is no more reason for doubting that this omission was in accord with the desires of Governor Winthrop, who negotiated the charter, than there is for doubting that the omission, coupled as it was with full guarantees of self-government, left the orthodox Puritans of Connecticut full freedom to pursue their own restrictive religious policies. The term religious freedom, as New Jersey's early history was to demonstrate again, needs to be read by the modern American with more regard for subtle differences in meaning which the peculiar circumstances of history have given it at different times.

That the favor shown the Puritan colonies by the Restoration government in its earliest years reflected some awareness of the assistance they might render in a conquest of New Netherland seems to be evident enough on the face of the record. The problem of Dutch competition obviously claimed close attention from men who were in a position to shape government policy. Obviously, too, the continued existence of New Netherland, so advantageously situated as it was with reference to the trade of all the English colonies, could not long be tolerated. Finally, when the decision was made to move against New Netherland, the plan called for an assault based upon New England.

To sum up thus is to run the risk of suggesting that policy followed a more consistent course of development than was actually the case. In truth, the government at Whitehall was still very poorly equipped to handle the colonial questions it faced. Hardly more than the very first steps had been taken toward creating administrative agencies of the type that modern empires have depended upon for the purposes of informed and co-ordinated action. Consequently, competing pressures on the existing centers of power within the government of Charles II brought about more than one example of inconsistency. Outranking all other centers of power, of course, was the royal court, where courtiers contended for the favor of the king and of those most obviously enjoying royal favor, much as they had in the days of Sir Walter Raleigh at Queen Elizabeth's court.

Fortunately, the number of especially influential men who became interested in the colonies, and who accordingly must be kept in mind by students of American history, is small. In fact, it is almost enough simply to name the six men Sir John Colleton, the Barbadian planter, managed to enlist in the Carolina project.* The Duke of Albemarle, formerly General Monk, one of Cromwell's major-generals, had played a leading role in effecting the return of the king to the throne in 1660. Edward Hyde, Earl of Clarendon, after long years of exile and until his fall from power in 1667, was the ranking minister of the restored king. Anthony Ashley Cooper, later Earl of Shaftesbury and leader of the Whig opposition to Charles II in the second half of the reign, was an especially astute politician who had sided with Parliament during the Civil War but had escaped

* Colleton himself and Sir William Berkeley were included in the Carolina charter of 1663 to make a total of eight proprietors. But neither of these two had an influence at all comparable to that of the others. Both men were active chiefly on the American side of the water, and owed whatever weight they could swing in London very largely to relatives and friends enlisted in their behalf.

too close an identification thereafter with Cromwell. William, Earl of Craven, from first to last, even to the hopeless stand he made for James II at the time of the Revolution of 1688, was an unqualified royalist who repeatedly found opportunities for personal advantage in his record of loyalty. John Lord Berkeley, soon to become one of the Jersey proprietors, after fighting for Charles I in the Civil War, had become the special companion in exile of the Duke of York, brother to Charles II and, after 1685, king himself as James II. Sir George Carteret, also soon to be a proprietor of New Jersey and the one responsible for its name, had commanded ships of the king before the Civil War. An expert seaman, described by Clarendon as the greatest seaman of his age among Englishmen, he had recaptured his native isle of Jersey from Parliamentary forces in 1643 and had held it for eight years thereafter as a base for the harassment of Parliamentary shipping and as a refuge for royalist exiles. Among those he entertained there was Prince Charles, later Charles II. To Carteret Charles had written in 1649, the year of his father's execution: "Carteret, I will add this to you under my own hand that I can never forget the good services you have done to my father and to me and if God bless me you shall find I do remember them to the advantage of you and yours."*

* Quoted in Charles M. Andrews, *The Colonial Period of American History* (4 vols.; New Haven, 1934-1938), III, 187 n.

Hardly less important than the influence these men enjoyed at court were the close associations of several of them with the administration of the Royal Navy, over which the Duke of York presided as Lord High Admiral of England. Berkeley held an influential place at the Admiralty, and Carteret, who was vice-chamberlain of the royal household, served too as treasurer of the navy. It may be worth adding, for future reference, that it was the navy which gave William Penn his special entry to the courts of Charles II and James II, for Penn's father served King Charles at sea as formerly he had served Cromwell.

York, Albemarle, Clarendon, Craven, Shaftesbury, Berkeley, and Carteret—these seven men are met with again and again, singly or in varying combinations, as the leaders of enterprises intended to strengthen England's position at sea, in America, and on the coasts of Africa. The list includes the proprietors, in addition to Carolina, of New York, New Jersey, and the Bahamas. It includes, too, leading adventurers in the organization of the Royal African Company and the Hudson's Bay Company. These same men are also found serving on various committees, *ad hoc* and more permanent, established from time to time to advise the government on the inseparable problems of trade and colonies. Fortunately situated in the main centers of power in Restoration England, and charged with heavy public responsibilities, they were especially alert to strategic considerations that would govern the outcome of an increasingly acute contest with Holland for supremacy in the rapidly developing trade of the Atlantic basin. Their initial effort, in Carolina, was directed against the old enemy Spain, but the greatest of their achievements came in the conquest of Dutch New Netherland.

II

PURITANS IN NEW JERSEY

Plans for the English conquest of New Netherland had their origin in the office of the Duke
of York, Lord High Admiral, where Berkeley and
Carteret enjoyed great influence. Drafted and executed at a time when England and Holland were
not only at peace but were engaged in continuing
negotiations for the settlement of their differences,
the plans repeatedly have provoked New York's
historians to extended exclamations of moral in-
dignation. Comment upon the question here can
be limited, for a full discussion would require
comment upon the morality, not of a particular
group of men, nor of a particular nation, but
of the age itself. The English conquest of New
Netherland was well enough in line with the common practices of the time. It would be a while
yet before it could be said that the "peace of
Europe" reached out to embrace all of the remote
frontiers of trade and settlement on which representatives of the several European states contended
for advantage. One can wish that New York's
historians, and especially those who in the nine-

teenth century labored so diligently in her behalf, had been less concerned to cultivate the State's understandable pride in its Dutch origins and more interested in understanding the dominant event in its history. That event, of course, was the English conquest of 1664.

As the record stands, we know all too little of that enterprise, no doubt in significant part because it developed as a military operation which had to be protected against the prying eyes of Dutch agents in London. The plan obviously was drafted with great care to maintain secrecy, and in no way were the planners more successful than in the "cover plan," as modern military men would describe it, that was suggested by Lord Clarendon's increasing annoyance over the situation in New England. Massachusetts had continued to equivocate in its responses to the king's lenient proposals. Moreover, the Connecticut charter had precipitated a bitter quarrel with Rhode Island over possession of the western bank of Narragansett Bay, and an even more bitter contest between Connecticut and New Haven. The latter had led a separate jurisdiction embracing a number of associated towns both on the mainland and Long Island, but all of these had been incorporated into Connecticut under the provisions of its charter of 1662, with results which ultimately included a significant migration into New Jersey by men bitterly unreconciled to Connecticut's final victory. More immediately, the quarrel between these two Puritan communities brought to London additional evidence of a situation that obviously called for investigation and report, and this at a time when Colonel Richard Nicolls was soon to sail from England for an attack upon New Netherland from New England.

In the circumstances, what could be more natural than the decision to place Colonel Nicolls also at the head of a commission for investigation of the situation in New England? Judged both by political and military considerations, the wisdom of this decision is debatable, to say the least, for there was an obvious conflict of interest in the double mission assigned to Nicolls. It is not surprising that the investigation subsequently undertaken in New England had most disappointing results, partly because Nicolls was too busy in New York to give it the leadership needed, but the point that counts here is that the commission for the investigation covered the military operation perfectly. After surrendering, Peter Stuyvesant recalled bitterly that he had been advised by his superiors in Holland, while Nicolls was at sea, to have no fear because the sole purpose of the expedition was to bring New England into submission to the authority of the Anglican bishops.

Nicolls was an exceptionally able man and the first in a long line of military men to serve as governor of an English colony in North America. He began his military career in the king's service during the Civil War. Subsequently, he went into exile, where he increased his experience as a soldier under York's command in the French Wars of the Fronde. He returned home in 1660 as a member of the Duke of York's household, and until his death in 1672, on board a man-of-war at the Battle of Soleby early in the third Anglo-Dutch war, he remained in the Duke's service. When he sailed from England in May, 1664, his command included three men-of-war, a transport, all four the king's own, and three hundred or more troops who had been recruited in the service of the Duke of York, some, it appears, on assurance that they would receive land grants in the area they were to conquer. Such additional force as Nicolls might require was to be recruited in New England, or rather, to be solicited from the English colonies there. Having completed the military operation, he was to become governor over an extraordinary collection of territories granted the Duke of York by royal charter early in the preceding March.

It is customary to speak of that charter as the New York Charter, but this designation is quite misleading as to its full content. Granted to York with powers of government as lord proprietor were all the lands lying between the Delaware and Connecticut Rivers, together with Long Island, Nantucket, Martha's Vineyard, and the extensive area running from the upper coast of Maine all the way to the St. Lawrence River. Considerations of space forbid any attempt here to discuss all of

the intriguing questions presented by these aston-
ishing bounds. One can be certain only that the
main objective was to give the Duke of York title
to, and adequate rights of jurisdiction over, the
entire area theretofore included in the claims of
the Dutch West India Company for its province
of New Netherland. Use of the Delaware River to
fix the western boundary left out, it is true, the
Dutch and Swedish settlements in that valley, virtually all of which were on the far side of the river,
but the promptness with which Nicolls moved
against the Delaware settlements, after winning
control of the Hudson, leaves no room for doubt
that the plan was to seize the whole of New
Netherland. The Duke took title on the west bank
of the Delaware by right of conquest, and Nicolls
immediately placed the area under the government he had established at New York, as New
Amsterdam was promptly renamed. Perhaps the
omission of the west bank of the Delaware in the
charter is explained by a desire to avoid an immediate quarrel with Lord Baltimore, who was
in London, and who by his protest might have
brought about a breach of military security. Perhaps it was merely because the leaders of the
project well understood, from a long history, that
title by conquest could be as good as any other
type of title.

It is possible that the eastward extension of
York's bounds from the Hudson to the Connecticut River, which incorporated most of the settled

area of the Connecticut colony, bespeaks some inclination on the part of the King's government to reconsider its recent action in issuing the Connecticut charter. But it is more likely that the New York charter, which is known to have been very hastily drafted, simply followed the obvious bounds of previously asserted Dutch claims, which had included the Connecticut Valley. A settlement of conflicting English claims there could be negotiated, as soon they were, once the Duke's title to whatever the Dutch had claimed was established.

Of greater interest to students of New Jersey's history, surprisingly, is the off-shore extension of the grant to include Long Island, Nantucket, Martha's Vineyard, and then, back on shore, the upper Maine coast. This extension, which fortunately has no modern survival beyond the attachment of Long Island to the State of New York, made no more sense politically than it did geographically. Geography, of course, provided warrant enough for linking Long Island with New York, as did also the fact that the Dutch claimed it as a part of New Netherland. But in 1664, and for many years thereafter, Long Island was actually an extension of Puritan New England; and Nantucket, Martha's Vineyard, and Maine could never have been anything more than useless appendages to a colony having its main seat on Manhattan Island. The explanation evidently must be sought in complicated negotiations involving a purchase John Lord Berkeley had made, in 1662, of the

Earl of Stirling's title to Long Island and Maine, together with other islands lying off the intervening coastline, under a grant Stirling's father had received from the long-since defunct New England Council. Berkeley had been unsuccessful in attempts to secure royal confirmation of this purchase. The Duke of York, apparently, showed more willingness to accommodate his friend. Whatever the full facts, and here as at so many places the record is incomplete, the Stirling title seems to have been a major consideration not only in determining the extraordinary bounds established in the New York charter but in the Duke of York's subsequent transfer of a half-interest in New Jersey to Berkeley. It is possible to be certain of one point only. If the Duke of York agreed to deed away half of New Jersey for the off-shore islands and the upper part of Maine, he made a very poor bargain.

Colonel Nicolls, a far more sensible man than his patron the Duke, moved with good fortune and marked skill to the quick accomplishment of his original mission. The Puritans at Boston, where he first landed, were cautious and somewhat cool in their reception, having had advance reports of his commission to look into their affairs. He, in turn, was diplomatic and obviously inclined to put first things first. His stay was short, for at Boston he heard that the Connecticut Puritans had won all of Long Island, which was true enough. Accordingly, he determined to move at once against New

Amsterdam. On reaching Gravesend late in August, 1664, he was joined by Governor Winthrop of Connecticut and by auxiliary troops drawn chiefly, no doubt, from the Puritan towns of Long Island. But he had little need for this or other auxiliary support. With his three men-of-war he easily blockaded the entrance to the great harbor, a blockade made firm by a detachment of troops put ashore on Staten Island to seize and hold Dutch gun emplacements there. Quickly, he followed up with a blockade of New Amsterdam itself, where Stuyvesant was poorly equipped to fight and found no willingness among his people to fight. The early surrender of New Amsterdam sealed the doom of Fort Orange, which also surrendered without resistance and took the name of Albany. Only on the Delaware River did the English invaders find a contest on their hands. They won, and with control of the Hudson and the Delaware there came possession of what was soon to be known as New Jersey.

Everywhere the terms of surrender offered by Nicolls were generous. Only in the plundering by Sir Robert Carr's victorious troops on the Delaware did the English risk their hope that the inhabitants of New Netherland might be persuaded to continue as residents of the new proprietorship. The principal guarantees were that existing titles in property would be confirmed for all inhabitants who swore allegiance to the King of England, and that all would have freedom of worship according to accustomed usages. Even Peter Stuyvesant, after returning to Holland for the purpose of clearing the record on his administration and defense of New Netherland, elected to live out the short remainder of his life on Manhattan Island.

Nicolls located his government and the major part of the English garrison at New York. Detachments of troops were stationed at Albany, below that point at Kingston, where the Esopus empties into the Hudson, and on the Delaware. He was fully alert to the prospect that open warfare with Holland might come at any time. Formal hostilities actually began in the spring of 1665 and were ended only in 1667. Accordingly, he was prompt in the attention he gave to the possibilities for a development of the area that would strengthen England's position there, and equally prompt in recognizing the central importance of New Jersey.

In a letter to the Earl of Clarendon, written in the spring of 1665, Nicolls reported several acute observations regarding his conquest. He dismissed Maine, Martha's Vineyard, and Nantucket Island as of no use to the Duke's new estate. He considered the soil of Connecticut and of Long Island to be of poor quality, and described the winter season on the Hudson as too cold for that valley to attract more than a few settlers. The main hope of building up the English population and rounding out the economy of the new province lay across the Hudson in New Jersey. This letter expressed his great disappointment on receiving the news that

New Jersey had been granted to Berkeley and Carteret, but there is no reason for doubt that it accurately reflected his carefully considered judgment. As late as 1669 we find him attempting to persuade the Duke of York that he had made a serious mistake in deeding away New Jersey. What is more to the point, virtually his every act between the fall of 1664 and the spring of 1665, a period through which he labored either in ignorance of the grant his patron had made in the preceding June or in the hope that the original decision might be reconsidered, supports the conclusion that his letter to Clarendon accurately described the considerations which had shaped his own policies.

As early as December 1664, Nicolls entered into an agreement with Governor Winthrop by which the Duke's claim to a jurisdiction extending to the Connecticut River was surrendered in return for Connecticut's surrender of its claim to Long Island. The boundary agreed upon ran very close to the line dividing the states of New York and Connecticut today. Although it cannot be said that this agreement finally settled the question either of that boundary or of the Duke's claim to a jurisdiction reaching to the Connecticut River, it did put an end to Connecticut's attempts to govern Long Island and it also significantly indicated Nicolls' willingness to accept a compromise settlement of issues which, unresolved, could only weaken the English community in a renewed contest with the Dutch. Although he had, as we have seen, no great estimate of Long Island's worth, he was fully alert to the opportunity that island offered as a recruiting ground for the settlement of New Jersey. Almost immediately after the conquest of New Amsterdam some of the Long Island Puritans had opened negotiations, in September, 1664, with Nicolls for the purpose of getting a grant for settlement across the bay on the Jersey shore. He agreed that they might proceed on a condition destined to become basic in the land policies of both New Jersey and New York, which was that the petitioners first clear the Indians' title to the area they desired. This having been accomplished, to his own satisfaction at least, he issued on December 1, 1664, his first major grant of land in New Jersey to a group of Puritans hailing mainly from Long Island—the Elizabethtown Grant, as it has commonly been known. It was a generous grant, reaching southward from the Passaic River to the Raritan River and inland for a considerable distance.

A further, and highly significant, step in the development of Nicolls' policy for strengthening the English position in what had been New Netherland came at Hempstead, on Long Island, in February, 1665. There he promulgated, before, an assembly of representatives from the English and Dutch towns of Long Island and Westchester, a remarkable document known to history as the Duke's Laws. They would be better described as

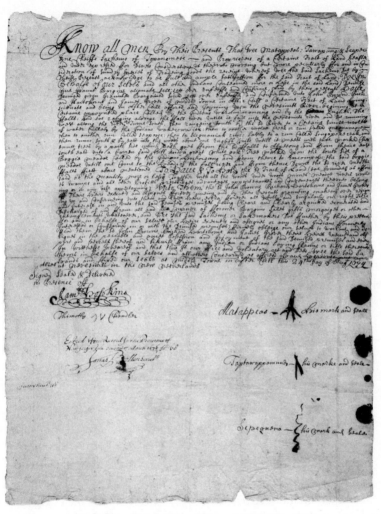

An Indian Deed, New Jersey, August 24, 1674
Courtesy of the Princeton University Library

Nicolls' Laws, for there is little reason for believing that the Duke of York contributed much on this occasion beyond the latitude that a long-trusted retainer assumed he had been allowed. Whatever the truth may be on that point, the document is of the first importance for an understanding of the history of all the middle colonies, and so of the history of the United States of America.

The Duke's Laws had immediate force only in newly-created King's County, which embraced Staten Island, Long Island, and Westchester. The county was to be divided into three ridings, and in each riding local administration was entrusted to a court of sessions made up of magistrates drawn from residents of the community, an arrangement very similar to that upon which the English depended in England, on the Chesapeake, and in New England, and not too markedly dissimilar from the practices to which the Dutch villages of New Netherland had been accustomed. The town meeting, the distinctive political institution of Puritan New England and then of the English settlers on Long Island, received no formal recognition, but neither was it prohibited, and the inhabitants of very town and village were given the right to choose their own officers. That right carried the substance of the right to local self-government, and for many years after 1665 the Long Island Puritans continued to depend upon the familiar practices of their town meetings. Provisions governing legal rights and procedures drew heavily upon the usages of the English common law, but they also incorporated significant adaptations suggested by the experience, and legislation, of the New England colonies. On the critical question of religious worship, Nicolls' code required that each community build and support a church of its own choice, a requirement giving as much protection to the Reformed Church in the Dutch villages as it did to the Puritan congregations in the more numerous English towns.

In thus Anglicizing immediately the administration of that part of his province in which the population was overwhelmingly English, Nicolls undoubtedly intended to assure any Englishmen who might be considering a move into the province that they could live there from the first under familiar laws and institutions. In other words, here was a promise that King's County, with its high sheriff and a deputy sheriff in each riding, and with local courts manned by resident justices of the peace, was only the first of other such counties that might be created. No additional counties were established by him, but the general scheme he had in mind is suggested by the provisions found in his second major grant of land in New Jersey. This has been known to history as the Monmouth Grant. Dated in April, 1665, the Monmouth patent covered the acreage lying between the Raritan River and Barnegat Bay, with a generous extension inland. To the Monmouth patentees, who again were led by Long Island Puritans, Nicolls conceded every necessary guarantee of local self-government, except the right to ignore the Duke's Laws.

There is also good reason for believing that Governor Nicolls expected that his code would provide a pattern of law and government that might be extended in time to cover all the Dutch and Swedish communities of the province. Indeed, this substantially is what happened over a course of years. Except for New York City, which in 1665 was converted to an English scheme of government by mayor and alderman, Dutch communities lying outside King's County continued to be governed by their own local courts, according to long established usage, but under the watchful eye of the nearest English military commander. At Bergen in Jersey, up the Hudson at Kingston and Albany, and on the west bank of the Delaware, the transition from Dutch to English law and procedure was accomplished by a gradual process that became complete, over the years, at different times at different places. Last of all to complete the transition was the court at Albany, where the English were disinclined to interfere with a profitable trade with the Iroquois Indians which long had been conducted by resident Dutch merchants. Although Richard Nicolls was denied an opportunity to superintend the change-over beyond its very earliest stages, he must be credited as the author of policies which effected in time a generally satisfactory transition from Dutch to English rule in what formerly had been New Netherland.

The distinguishing feature of those policies gave time to every Dutch community for adjustment to English procedures, and simultaneously it held out the prospect that any community of Englishmen could expect to be governed immediately by English law. No less worthy of special comment is the provision for religious freedom. Too often, for the purposes of the historian, the modern American has thought of that freedom in terms wholly of the individual's right to follow his own conscience. Nicolls thought rather, as did other promoters of settlement in America during the Restoration era, in terms of a right belonging to each community to follow its own convictions—except of course for William Penn, who placed the right of the individual first. Whatever else needs to be said about that policy, which guarded the rights of the Reformed and Lutheran inhabitants of the area as well as it did the rights of any English group, it was an ingenious device for promoting immigration from New England, where so many men cherished the freedom they had found in America to maintain their own form of Puritan orthodoxy, as other men cherished their individual freedom of conscience.

When Nicolls wrote to Clarendon in the spring of 1665, he had recently returned from the Boston area, where at Cambridge he had secured the printing of a broadside advertising, for one and all,

"The Conditions for New Planters in the Territories of his Royal Highness the Duke of York." These conditions were altogether consistent with those already stipulated in the Elizabeth and Monmouth grants, and with the principles set forth in the Duke's Laws. The Indian title must be cleared by purchase. It was expected that settlement would be undertaken in town communities. Each town would be free to follow its own religious preference. Election by the inhabitants of local officers, military and civil, was assured, as also was the right to enact local ordinances governing "small causes." For a five-year period after settlement, all members of the community were to be exempt from taxation by higher authority, and thereafter they would be subject only to "the public rates and payments." Whether or not this phrasing was intended to include the quit-rents specified in both the Elizabeth and Monmouth grants is debatable. Perhaps Governor Nicolls must be charged with some vagueness on a question of rents which the New Englanders were generally unaccustomed to pay, and which was destined to cause great trouble during the years ahead for New Jersey. The governor was much encouraged by the early response he found to this promotional effort, but the news he received on returning to New York put an end to his high hopes. Thereafter, the agents of John Lord Berkeley and Sir George Carteret were in control of the area Nicolls had selected for settlement by English colonists.

The more one puzzles over the Duke of York's grant to Berkeley and Carteret the more puzzling it becomes. Obviously, the news of it came as a great disappointment, if not complete surprise, to one of the Duke's most trusted and able lieutenants, one who had been privy to the original plans for the conquest of New Netherland and who had carried those plans out most successfully. Obviously, too, the Duke had acted without waiting for a report from his lieutenant; the grant was made in June, when Nicolls had been at sea a month and was almost two months away from completing his original assignment. The grant made no sense at all in terms of the strategic considerations which had led to the conquest of New Netherland, and which guided Nicolls in his plans for the development of the area. On the seriously truncated New York jurisdiction, reduced now, as New Netherland had been in Stuyvesant's day, to widely separated spheres on the Delaware and the Hudson, the Jersey grant imposed a serious handicap that resulted in a chronic state of financial embarrassment. In years not too far ahead, that embarrassment would complicate, during the opening rounds of the great contest with France for dominance on the North American continent, the relations of the imperial government with every English colony in North America from Virginia northward. To put the point briefly, New York never had the capacity to meet the cost of its own defense, and this at a time when the defense of New York, and more particularly of Albany, was of the most critical importance to England's interests in North America. Moreover, by deeding the land between the Hudson and the Delaware to the two Jersey proprietors without an affirmative grant of political jurisdiction, the Duke of York introduced into the history of New Jersey an element of uncertainty destined to disturb its political life for almost forty years thereafter.

The New Jersey grant was in the form of a deed of lease and release which conveyed title in the soil, but none of the jurisdictional rights previously awarded the Duke of York by royal charter, in accordance with the usual stipulations made in behalf of other proprietors holding colonial lands by royal grant. Even so, Berkeley and Carteret were permitted to act, from the first, on an assumption that they held full political powers over the New Jersey area. Not until almost a decade had passed did the Duke of York, so far as an imperfect record shows, question the authority of the government established by the proprietors of New Jersey, when in the summer of 1665, they sent out Philip Carteret, Sir George's cousin, with a commission to serve as their governor. Governor Carteret landed at Elizabethport in August of that year with credentials which Nicolls, despite his disappointment, failed to challenge. Thus was New Jersey, or New Caesaria, as the proprietors also designated their province, launched upon its separate and frequently troubled course.

It has often been assumed by historians that the Duke of York was a representative proprietor of his time, that his primary interest in New York was to establish for himself a personal estate in North America. But that assumption can hardly be reconciled with his quick decision to deed away, well in advance of the time at which he could have expected a report from his agent in America, the lands which were best suited for the development of a rent-producing estate. The plain and undisputed facts would seem to argue rather that, at least in the beginning, he was indifferent to all considerations except the need to get the Dutch out of North America. Once provision had been made for accomplishing that end, he apparently was guided chiefly by a willingness to accommodate his friends, and this without much thought for the consequence of what he did. Later, and especially after the Dutch had reconquered the area in 1673, he may have had some second thoughts, but even then his actions were variable enough to suggest a continuing indifference to interests which other proprietors placed first. It is difficult to avoid the conclusion that the Duke of York's activity in North America sprang chiefly from considerations of state, and that of those considerations he had at best an imperfect understanding.

Lord Berkeley and Sir George Carteret, the chief beneficiaries of his short-sightedness, as previously noted, were in every way representative of the colonial proprietors of their day. It was their hope that they might find, at no great cost to their existing estates, a profitable property in America. As the Earl of Shaftesbury subsequently remarked of the Carolina proprietors, their personal interest in the venture was not that of a merchant, but rather of a landlord. The pattern they followed was one set much earlier by Lord Baltimore in Maryland, where in keeping with ancient medieval usages the proprietor's title to the soil was joined with broad rights of jurisdiction over its inhabitants, who in turn held their lands from the proprietor in return for a stipulated rent. Of the two New Jersey proprietors, Carteret seems to have been the one most willing to make an investment for the development of the estate. At any rate, most of the thirty or more persons accompanying Governor Carteret to New Jersey in 1665 apparently had sailed on his cousin's account, and it is only just that the name of the State should still perpetuate the fame he had won as a loyal subject of his king. Governor Carteret bought rights in the Elizabeth Grant and promptly took over the job, perforce surrendered to him by Governor Nicolls, of encouraging the migration of New Englanders into New Jersey.

For the accomplishment of that purpose he had come well provided with the Concessions and Agreement of 1665, a document which deserves to be better known among Americans than it is. The original had been drafted by the Carolina proprietors in response to a request from Sir John Yeamans in Barbados for a full statement of the conditions upon which settlement in Carolina might be undertaken. The Carolina proprietors sealed the document under the date of January 7, 1665. The New Jersey proprietors revised the document only in minor details and dated it February 10, 1665. Subsequently, they entrusted this version to the hands of Governor Carteret, who published it throughout New England soon after his arrival in New Jersey.

That he should have done so was no accident, for the paper, quite obviously, had been drafted originally to attract the New England Puritans. Why this should have been the intent of a document issued in response to a specific request from the Barbadian adventurers is a question not too easy to answer, but the fragmentary evidence suggests several possibilities. There is some reason for believing that the Barbadian adventurers may have had New England associates, perhaps merchants trading to the island. It is also possible that the proprietors may have been negotiating with two separate associations of prospective adventurers to Carolina, one of Barbadians and the other of New Englanders. We know very little of this except for incidental references the proprietors made to their New England correspondents and the fact that in 1663, when the Barbadian planters sent William Hilton on an exploratory voyage along the Carolina coast, a group of New

Englanders actually landed with cattle on the Cape Fear River, in modern North Carolina. As it happened, these men quickly departed the river, leaving behind both the cattle and a posted notice of warning to all others who might consider settlement in that latitude, a notice Hilton indignantly tore down on another exploratory voyage in 1664. But the hope of attracting other New Englanders to Carolina persisted. Perhaps it was because the Puritan settlement of New England was generally viewed at the time of the Restoration as an especially successful colonizing venture. Even Governor William Berkeley, on his return to Virginia in 1662, had been advised by his instructions to consider New England as a model for emulation on the Chesapeake, no doubt to his chagrin.

It is just possible, though by no means provable, that the Concessions and Agreement was originally drafted with a view to the double use to which it subsequently was put. The best support for such an interpretation lies in the fact that Berkeley and Carteret, who were deeply involved in the project for a conquest of New Netherland and who thus could be expected to be especially well informed on the situation in New England, were in position to have influenced fundamentally the original draft of the document. But these are points for the scholar to debate. What counts is that the document was made to serve both the Carolina and the New Jersey ventures, and that thereby it becomes peculiarly representative of the Restoration phase of English colonization in North America.

Fortunately, "The Concessions and Agreement of the Lords Proprietors of New-Caesaria, or New Jersey, to and with all such as shall Settle or Plant there" may be read in its entirety in another volume in the Tercentenary Series. Here it will be enough to note its principal provisions.

The headright of 150 acres promised for every freeman and "able man servant" going to the colony in the "first voyage" had little immediate practical meaning in the case of New Jersey, except for those accompanying Governor Carteret and, perhaps, as a rough measurement for the award of land to those migrating from New England. The downward graduation of the headright according to the year of migration, from 150 acres to 60 acres in 1667, was in keeping with promotional practices which in the past had consistently given special recognition to the hardships the original settlers of any area must endure. Typical, too, was the provision that lesser grants would be made for the migration of "weaker servants"—roughly speaking, women and children—and that servants, on the expiration of their term of servitude, would be entitled to a land grant of their own. This last was a device often depended upon by the promoters of new colonies to overcome the advantages naturally belonging to the older settlements. These provisions probably should be read by the student of New Jersey's history with attention not so much to the specific details as to the liberal standard they set for the distribution of land. In the actual settlement of New Jersey still more generous standards obtained. There can be little doubt that land-hunger, above all, was the motivating force in the settlement of New Jersey.

This observation is in no way intended to detract from the very great significance of the religious guarantees provided by the Concessions and Agreement. All prospective immigrants into the colony were assured that no attempt would be made to enforce conformity with an Anglican church establishment. Instead, each community was given the right to make its own provision for religious worship, provided it did not deny the "Liberty besides to any person or persons to keepe and maintayne what Preachers or Ministers they please." The qualification needs to be read closely, for it undoubtedly was intended to provide something less than a full gurantee of liberty of conscience, interpreted as Roger Williams had interpreted it and as the modern American has come to understand it. Although the Restoration era brought marked progress toward the achievement of full religious freedom in the colonies, men were still reluctant to surrender an assumption that public authority had an obligation for the support of religion, if only because religion was considered to be a main prop for any acceptable social order. The most important advance at this time was toward a greater freedom of choice in determining the religious organization, or organizations, which were entitled to receive public support. The New Jersey proprietors probably intended to do no more than establish the right of the inhabitants of a community to organize themselves into more than one congregation. Given the tendency New Englanders had shown toward settlement in communities made congenial by the religious convictions its members shared, this part of the Concessions and Agreement is best read as a shrewdly conceived invitation to orthodox Puritans, Baptists, Quakers, and whatever other group one might find cause to mention, to think of establishing communities of their own in New Jersey.

Additional assurances, in this matter of religion, are found in the provisions for government. All men, on taking an oath of allegiance to the King and of faithfulness to the proprietors, were to become freemen of the province, with full and equal rights. None of their civic rights could be abridged because of "any difference in opinion or practice in matters of Religious concernements," except as a penalty for actual disturbance of the "civill peace." For students of American constitutional history there is special interest in the self-denying provision by which the proprietors bound themselves, and their heirs, never to abridge the guarantees of religious freedom there established.

The province was to be administered by a governor appointed by the proprietors, a council of six to twelve men appointed by the governor, and a general assembly, meeting annually. This general assembly included the governor, the council, and elected representatives of the freemen. It was given very full powers, which were limited chiefly by a prohibition of statutes contrary to the laws of England or in violation of the Concessions and Agreement, especially its provisions governing religion. The assembly's powers, let it be noted, included the authority to provide for the appointment and maintenance of clergymen, so long as it was understood that any group might maintain "what Preachers or Ministers they please." In addition, the assembly, which first met in 1668, was empowered to establish courts, to legislate on the agencies and forms of local government, to fix fees and salaries, to assess taxes, except on undeveloped land of the proprietors, and even to enact legislation governing the distribution of land. All told, the Concessions and Agreement of 1665 constitutes a remarkably signficant commentary both on the conditions Englishmen in America were prepared to accept in occupying a new area, and on the willingness of the Restoration proprietors to do all they could to meet those conditions.

On one point only were the proprietors uncompromising. That was in their insistence on the payment of quit-rents, after the lapse of a few years allowed for all new settlers. The quit-rent was a familiar feature of the land system in England, where it had taken its name many, many years before from the fact that by payment of a monetary rent to the landlord the tenant was freed, or quit, from other obligations to his lord. It had been introduced into English America by the Virginia Company, at the same time that it introduced the headright, and outside New England, and even in some parts of New England, it had become by now a conventional obligation imposed upon most land grants. From the point of view of the proprietors, of course, this was the sum and substance of their entire enterprise, for their basic purpose was to promote the development of a rent-producing estate in New Jersey. But for all their acute understanding of the New Englander, including many of his special prejudices and convictions, they overlooked, or else felt it safe to ignore, one of the most important of his prejudices. In most parts of New England, the Puritan settler had grown used to having no landlord, for it was the general custom of the Puritan jurisdictions to deed land subject only to the payment of public levies or taxes. The Puritan in America was not only strongly inclined to guard his freedom on questions of religion; he was also strongly disinclined to pay tribute to any man for the land he himself had cleared and developed. In short, he disliked paying rents, and he had quickly come to hold a view of title in real property that was in fundamental conflict with the main objective of the New Jersey proprietors.

There was trouble ahead, of course, serious

trouble, and it began as early as 1670, when the first rents fell due. For two years thereafter the colony was in a state of turmoil. The story is tangled and imperfectly documented. Fortunately, no account is required here. It is signficant that the main seat of the trouble lay in the areas granted, previous to August 1665, by Governor Nicolls to the Elizabeth and Monmouth patentees. Both of those grants had stipulated that quit-rents would be payable to the Duke of York, but the deeds predated the promulgation of the Concessions and Agreement, and Governor Carteret may have suffered from inexperience in his subsequent negotiations with the Puritan patentees. The Puritan could be a shrewd bargainer, quick to turn the skills he had acquired in the discussion of theological questions to his advantage in an effort to win a point at law. In this instance, the protesting Puritans seem to have been, technically at any rate, in the wrong, and they were ultimately to lose the argument. Quit-rents were payable through many years thereafter in New Jersey, as in most other American colonies. This bitter dispute is important primarily for its revelation of the difficulty inherent in any attempt to fit the New England Puritan into a proprietary scheme of colonial settlement. He held too many stubborn convictions regarding his own rights, and so it was he who first cast the politics of colonial New Jersey into a pattern of popular resistance to proprietary prerogative.

It was also the New England Puritan who placed the dominant stamp of his own peculiar convictions on New Jersey's first society. When Governor Carteret arrived, there seem to have been no more than four families living at Elizabeth. The Dutch living in and around Bergen may have numbered—men, women, and children—two hundred souls. The thirty or so settlers arriving with Carteret, mostly French-speaking people from the Channel Isles, brought not even the promise of a significantly large migration from across the Atlantic. But soon the New Englanders, acting on previously conceived plans or in accord with new arrangements with Governor Carteret and the original Elizabeth and Monmouth patentees, began to build their towns—at Elizabeth, at Woodbridge, at Piscataway, at Middletown, and at Shrewsbury. The people came from Long Island, Connecticut, Massachusetts, New Hampshire, and Rhode Island. From New Haven, Branford, Milford, and Guilford, beginning in 1666, came an especially devout and orthodox group of Puritans to build the town that in time would be known as Newark. Their zeal owed not a little to the fact that they were unreconciled to the final victory Connecticut had won in its effort to absorb the formerly separate New Haven jurisdiction. With no prospect of help from Governor Nicolls, who had a way of getting along with Governor Winthrop of Connecticut, and under pressure from Massachusetts and Plymouth to close ranks in the face of Nicolls's impending investigation of New England's affairs, the New Haven towns finally had surrendered to Connecticut. Among their inhabitants, however, there remained not a few whose view of this enforced union was that of the "unreconstructed" rebel. At Newark the most orthodox of Puritans were in control. At Piscataway the Baptists had the upper hand. And so it would go in New Jersey.

With the Puritan came the New England town. This was not exactly the compact community of New England's first years, but a community somewhat loosened in adjustments, long since begun, to the generous dimensions of even a small part of the North American continent. There was room enough for expanding ambitions in New Jersey; and for town perhaps there should be substituted, at the beginning, the term township which still describes a unit of government that is fundamental in the administrative and political life of the modern state. With the town, or township, came the town meeting, always an institution less dependent upon the rulings of higher authority than upon the political inclinations and habits of the people accustomed to its use. With the town came, too, the meetinghouse, its austere features bearing somber, but eloquent, testimony to some of the more important parts of an ancient Christian tradition against which the more extreme Protestants protested. It was not intended to be a church, not even a frontier substitute for a church. Rather, its purpose, as the name very accurately described it, was to provide a building in which the people might meet for civic as well as for religious purposes, though of course the latter ranked first.

Many other settlers, of widely differing religious persuasions, have followed the Puritans into New Jersey. The traces of a once-dominant Puritanism in the upper-half of the state become fainter with each passing year, but they may still be found. Perhaps in passing through some small village lying off the main road, and little touched as yet by modern development, one detects a similarity, either in the buildings or in their arrangement around the village square, to the New England town. Perhaps one notes that the laws of the State, in some particulars, continue to reflect essential features of the moral code by which the Puritan lived, as did his Dutch neighbor, who also was guided by a Calvinist tradition. Perhaps the occasion comes rather when a neighbor chooses a college for his son, or goes himself on vacation; if the neighbor can fulfill his heart's desire, he probably will take his vacation somewhere in New England.

Below Princeton, or Trenton, the orientation of life is different, for between these two communities one crosses the line which in colonial days separated East Jersey from West Jersey.

III

QUAKERS ON THE DELAWARE

THE FIRST STEP toward dividing the province into the two discrete territorial and political units of East Jersey and West Jersey was taken in 1674. That year brought an end to the third Anglo-Dutch war, during which the Dutch had recaptured New York and briefly re-established New Netherland. This restoration, dating from August, 1673, when a Dutch fleet up from a recent raid on English shipping in Virginia seized New York City, lasted only a few months and resulted in no long-run disturbance of the major arrangements previously made by Englishmen for the development of the area. When the English regained possession by the provisions of the Treaty of Westminister in 1674, however, legal considerations argued that all parties should seek appropriate confirmation of their former titles. Thus, the Duke of York sought and secured from his brother, King Charles II, a confirmation of the original New York charter, which was made with no change either in the bounds or of the powers it originally had conferred. Similarly, it became necessary for the New Jersey proprietors to secure confirmation of their grant from the Duke of York. In this requirement the province's division into East and West Jersey had its beginning.

It so happened that by 1674 John Lord Berkeley had lost interest. He had never been as active in the management of the province as Sir George Carteret, and for some time Berkeley's fortunes had been in decline. Perhaps the anti-rent agitations, which had immediately preceded the war and which could find no final settlement until after its end, had an influence on his decision. In any case, Berkeley sold his share in the Jersey proprietorship in March, 1674, to John Fenwick, acting in behalf of Edward Byllynge, both of them Quakers.

Whether because Byllynge's affairs were in a state of bankruptcy and confusion, or because he was soon involved in a bitter quarrel with his associate John Fenwick, or for other reasons, the Duke of York, while confirming Carteret's share in the New Jersey grant, failed to confirm the share sold by Berkeley. Indeed, not until 1680 did William Penn, who had been brought into the enterprise as early as 1674 to arbitrate the dispute between the Quaker associates, manage to secure the desired confirmation. Moreover, in confirming Carteret's half-share, the Duke of York deeded to him the upper half of the province, with a boundary, running from Barnegat Creek on the coast westward to the Delaware River, which actually gave to Carteret the larger "half" of the territory. In the attempt to get an adjustment of this inequity, Penn and other Quakers who, as trustees for Byllynge, had been drawn increasingly into a project for the establishment of a Quaker colony on the Delaware, negotiated with Carteret the "Quintipartite Deed" of July, 1676. By the terms of that agreement the line was rerun, from the east side of Little Egg Harbor, below Barnegat Bay, to the northwest corner of the province, thereby giving the Quakers the larger "half" of the territory and, what is more important, full possession of the eastern bank of the Delaware River. This division between East and West Jersey, as the two parts were called, was followed in the confirmation of title finally won by the West Jersey trustees from the Duke of York four years later.

The "Province Line," as the line of demarcation came to be known, represents much more than an arbitrary division between different claimants to the soil of New Jersey. Until the King took over the government of the province in 1702, there were two separate governments, each with its own governor and legislature. Even after 1702, though New Jersey then had a single governor, its legislature met alternately in Perth Amboy and Burlington, formerly the seats of government in East and West Jersey. For the historian, the Province Line marks a division between two distinct developments in the later phase of England's colonization

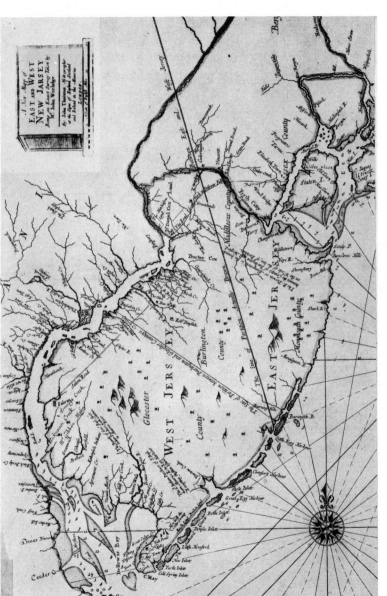

Detail from Map by John Thornton (c. 1700). *Courtesy of the Library of Congress and the Princeton University Press*

in North America. It also marks a division between two distinct but not wholly contrasting societies, the one predominantly Puritan in its origins, the other chiefly shaped at first by the ideals of the Quaker.

The Duke of York had done more in 1674 than give Carteret the greater share of the province. He actually had deeded to Carteret, perhaps justly in view of Carteret's superior record as a proprietor, the entire settled area of New Jersey. As late as 1672, George Fox, founder of the Society of Friends, had journeyed across West Jersey and described it as an unoccupied wilderness. It must be noted again that the Swedish, Finnish, and Dutch settlers on the Delaware had built their forts and opened up their farms on the west bank of the river. There were minor exceptions; across the river from New Castle in the Pennsville area, there were a few settlers, Swedes for the most part, but they were very few. In short, the eastern bank of the Delaware, which had cut among the rolling hills its own fertile and beautiful valley, one broadening out in its lower reaches to become a part of tide-water America, lay open for some new colonizing venture.

To that valley, and its tide-water extensions, came the Quaker, at first, it seems, simply to make there a profitable investment in good land, or to escape the bitter persecution which was his lot in Restoration England. But soon the opportunities of the Delaware Valley helped him to capture a vision inspiring the hope, so often identified with America, that he might build here a new society, better than any which existed in the old world.

The Quaker was a mystic, firmly persuaded, according to his doctrine of the "Inner Light," that man might enjoy fresh revelations of God's will. Not yet subject to the influence of "Quietism," which has so largely shaped the modern image of the Quaker, he was in these earlier days aggressively evangelical in his preaching. It often has been said that the Quakers abolished the priesthood, but it can just as well be said that Quakerism made every believer a priest. Any convert might feel a strong impulse to win other converts, and was qualified to undertake the mission, a fact which helps to explain the rapid spread of the movement, never large in numbers, throughout the British Isles and into the colonies. By 1660, only eight years after George Fox had founded the movement, Quaker missionaries had carried their message into every English colony in America, often to be welcomed as men welcome a plague and a pest. There were Quakers among the early settlers of East Jersey, but it was on the other side of the province that the Quakers found the opportunity which encouraged them to build a colony of their own.

Earliest of the Quaker settlements in West Jersey was that established at Salem late in 1675 under the leadership of John Fenwick, who was still at odds with Edward Byllynge and Byllynge's

scene in the Concessions and Agreements given by Byllynge's trustees to the settlers at Burlington.

The title of the document must have been intended to recall the basic charter Governor Carteret had brought from the proprietors to New Jersey in 1665. Certainly, the two documents had much in common, including a clause forbidding popularly elected assemblies to violate the basic guarantees provided therein for all members of the community. It is instructive for the modern American to observe that the emphasis in the Burlington Concessions fell most heavily upon the rights belonging to the individual in a court of law. Provisions intended to assure that the popular will would be expressed in the law enforced in court were very liberal indeed. The laws were to be enacted by annually elected assemblies depending for their authority upon a very popular franchise. As the trustees explained in simply eloquent terms: "There we lay a foundation for after ages to understand their liberty as men and christians, that they may not be brought in bondage, but by their own consent; for we put the power in the people." One hesitates to underscore the suggestion that a people can vote themselves into bondage, but there can be no doubt that the trustees were disinclined to place their full faith in the machinery of popular representation. Above all, they sought the ultimate protection of a concept of law so basically rooted in the inherent rights of the individual that no agency of the state, whether the legislature or a court of law, could override those rights. It would be difficult to think of any concept that is more important for modern Americans.

We know, as did the West Jersey trustees, that every man brought before a court of law is entitled to know the full charge against him, and to know it in sufficient time to prepare the best defense he can. We place our faith in the ancient procedures of the English jury, and in the need to protect the jury from browbeating by the judge. We allow the defendent a number of challenges to prospective jurors (though probably not quite so many as did the West Jersey trustees), lest the defendent be exposed to unfair risk. We know that all trials must be publicly conducted, lest our own rights be at some time dangerously compromised. And we know, if we have read the Burlington Concessions and Agreements, that our claim to these and other such protections is deeply rooted in the tradition which guides us as Americans.

William Penn may have deserved the credit for these provisions that has often been assigned to him. He himself had been jailed for his convictions, and he had been a central figure in a case establishing in English law a new independence of judgment for the jury. Moreover, the principles here set forth were consistent with the guarantees later enjoyed by his settlers in Pennsylvania. But there is just as good reason for attributing the authorship to Edward Byllynge, an otherwise undistinguished man, who seems to have made comparable proposals for the government of England in a pamphlet published as far back as 1659. The Quakers, generally, had come to embrace these views not only because they had originally been identified with the advanced thought of their age, but also out of their own bitter experience as members of a persecuted religious minority. It hardly need be added that at Burlington, as at Salem and elsewhere in West Jersey, every man was guaranteed the freedom of his conscience.

The Quaker, like the Puritan, worshiped in a meetinghouse, which at times might do double service by housing public agencies. Its simplicity, its plainness, bespoke, among other things, the plain and simple life every Quaker was supposed to live. For failing to observe that rule of life, and for other variations from a strict code of conduct, he might have to answer to his meeting, much as the Puritan for comparable offenses answered to his congregation. The Quaker was really very much a Puritan, despite sharp differences of conviction between the two, and the standard of morality and conduct set for West Jersey by its first settlers was not greatly different from that already established for East Jersey by the New Englanders. Nor was it any less enduring as an influence on the history of colony and state.

As the persecution of the Quakers increased during the closing years of Charles II's reign, they moved in growing numbers to West Jersey—all told, perhaps as many as one thousand seven hundred by 1682. An event of that year suggests the possibility that the movement also might have shaped significantly the further development of East Jersey. Sir George Carteret had died in 1680, and his share in the Jersey proprietorship was purchased in 1682 by a group of twelve men, all but one of them Quakers, a group which included Penn and others previously associated in the West Jersey trusteeship. Having now both West Jersey and a controlling voice in the management of East Jersey's affairs, the Quakers conceivably might have elected to concentrate all of their further efforts within the limits of New Jersey. Perhaps such a plan was considered, but it was never executed. Although the proprietors quickly gave their encouragement to a group of Scottish Quakers who planned a settlement in East Jersey, the project failed to achieve its full hopes. East Jersey was to receive very little of the impact of the great Quaker migration that was so soon to be channeled into Pennsylvania. Perhaps the Quaker leaders bought into the East Jersey proprietorship primarily for the purpose of covering the flank of a movement whose real objectives still lay along the Delaware.

Rivers at this time in American history, though they often served to mark political boundaries, are best viewed as highways which offered the migrating colonist easy access to the lands lying on both banks of the stream. The river, moreover, provided an easy means of communication from one bank to the other. In short, the natural thing was for a river to unite the people living along its course, and those who bothered to explore the opportunities it offered thought accordingly, unless some insuperable political barrier already had been erected.

With this point in mind, it is instructive to observe the sequence of certain developments in which William Penn played the central role. In 1680 he finally succeeded in getting from the Duke of York a confirmation of Byllynge's title to West Jersey. In that same year he made application for a grant in his own name to the area which became Pennsylvania. The Pennsylvania charter received its final seal in March, 1681, and in 1682 the Quaker settlement of Pennsylvania began. Finally, and in that same year, Penn secured from the Duke of York by deed of lease and release York's claim to title, by right of conquest, along that part of the western bank of the river which lay below Pennsylvania—the area, roughly, that is embraced by the modern state of Delaware. Thus, by 1682 William Penn had succeeded in establishing for the Quakers, either in Byllynge's name or his own, what was very close to full and clear title to the whole of the Delaware Valley, from Delaware Bay northward to New York. It was to be expected of course that Lord Baltimore, who also had a claim on the west bank of the Delaware, would protest, as promptly he did. But in the end, Penn's title proved to be the stronger, a fact to which the state of Delaware very largely owes its separate existence.

It has been assumed that Penn's decision to seek the grant of Pennsylvania reflected, in part at least, his dissatisfaction with the state of New Jersey's affairs. This may well be true. Fenwick's determination to pursue a separate course continued to make trouble for the Quaker venture. Not until 1683 were Byllynge's affairs in an order that permitted termination of the trusteeship, from which Penn himself had withdrawn in 1681. It must have been obvious, moreover, that the division of New Jersey into two parts was a potential source of continuing difficulty, and in 1680, when Penn first petitioned the king for his grant of Pennsylvania, there could be no assurance that the Quakers would gain the voice they subsequently acquired in the management of East Jersey. It can be conceded that these considerations may have counted heavily in the decision, but it is evident enough that the launching of Penn's new venture should not be viewed as an indication of a settled purpose to withdraw from the New Jersey venture. Not only did he become a proprietor of East Jersey in 1682, but in 1683 he became, by purchase of John Fenwick's rights, for the first time a proprietor of West Jersey.

However one may interpret Pennsylvania's origins, the story can be seen in its full dimensions only by viewing it as the climactic chapter in the history of England's colonizing efforts during the Restoration era. William Penn, it must be recognized, had every qualification for membership in the small group of proprietors who, after 1660, assumed the lead in attempts to extend England's possessions in North America, including the special influence he enjoyed at the royal court. Nor were his motives, despite a deep commitment to the goals inspiring fellow Quakers who entered into the venture with him, sharply different from those of the other proprietors. Pennsylvania was intended to be, in Penn's own words, a "Holy Experiment," but it was also intended to serve as an extension of the personal estate of Penn and his family. The chief difference, in comparison with other such estates established during the reign of Charles II, is that the Penn family managed to defend its proprietary rights all the way down to the American Revolution, a success matched only by that of the Lords Baltimore of Maryland.

Even the very liberal religious and political concessions William Penn made for the settlers of his province were less an innovation than a development of principles and practices which already had become a distinguishing feature of Restoration colonization. To this generalization some will feel that a decided exception must be made in the case of New York, which did not gain an undisputed right to a representative assembly until after the English Revolution of 1688. But long before that year the colonists living under

New York's jurisdiction, which prior to 1682 included the Dutch, Swedes, and Finns on the western bank of the Delaware, enjoyed freedom for separate forms of worship, protection of the individual's rights by enlightened laws, and the basic privilege of local self-government. It was Penn's role, as the last of the Restoration colonizers, to round out, to make more complete, what so frequently had been granted before. In fact, his own ideas for the government of Pennsylvania, as shown by the provisions he first made for it, were actually somewhat less liberal than those already written into the Burlington Concessions and Agreements of 1677. Similarly, the liberty of conscience guaranteed for the settlers of Pennsylvania represented no advance beyond the principle to which all of the Quaker settlements theretofore had been committed.

The most distinctive of William Penn's contributions to the colonization of North America was the encouragement he provided for the migration into his colony of non-English-speaking settlers from the European continent. At Germantown as early as 1683, recruits from the lower Rhineland, where Penn had twice visited as a Quaker missionary, had opened a new and extraordinarily significant chapter in the history of American immigration. Once more, however, it is necessary to observe that there was nothing exactly novel in the employment of people other than English, or British, for the purpose of strengthening England's position in North America. The pattern for Penn's policy of equal treatment for English and non-English settlers had been set by Richard Nicolls as early as 1665. Indeed, for some time after 1683 the largest number of alien settlers living within William Penn's own jurisdiction would be the Dutch, Swedes, and Finns who much earlier had occupied the lower reaches of the Delaware.

All this is in no way intended to detract from the very great significance of Pennsylvania's founding. The purpose, rather, is to suggest again the advantage that may be gained for an understanding of any part of the history of the middle colonies by seeing them as a whole. Certainly, no student of New Jersey's history after 1682 can safely fail to take into account the remarkable development of Pennsylvania.

As Pennsylvania quickly became the focal point for the highest hopes which brought the Quakers in increasing numbers to the New World, West Jersey both lost and gained. The new colony was somewhat like a magnet which drew in Quakers previously settled in the older colonies, often men who had enjoyed an advantageous experience in America. Among them were some of the merchants whose activity soon gave commercial importance to Philadelphia, and as city and colony prospered the power of the magnet increased. Nowhere was its pull more strongly felt than in West Jersey, which through many years continued to

MISSIVE
VAN
WILLIAM PENN,
Eygenaar en Gouverneur van
PENNSYLVANIA,
In AMERICA.

Geſchreven aan de Commiſſariſſen van de Vrye Societeyt der Handelaars op deſelve Provintie, binnen London reſiderende.

BEHELSENDE:

Een generale beſchrijvinge van de voornoemde Provintie : te weten / van hare Grondt / Lucht / Water / Saiſoenen en 't Product / ſoo uyt de natuur als door het bouwen / neffens de groote vermeerderinge of meenighvuldinge / welke het Land aldaar uytgevende is.

Als mede : van de Naturellen of Inboorlingen des Landts / haer Taal / Gewoontens en Manieren / haar Spijſen / Huyſen of Wigwams / Mildheyt / gemackelijcke manier van leven / Medicijnen / manieren van Begraaffenis / Godsdienſt / Offerhanden en Geſangen / haar Hooge-feeſten / Regeeringe / en ordre in hare Raden / wanneer ſy met yemandt handelen over het verkoopen van Landeryen / &c. Nevens hare Juſti-tie of Recht doen over quaatdoenders.

Mitsgaders een Bericht van de eerſte Coloniers de Hollanders / &c. En van de tegenwoordige toeſtant en weltgeſteltheyt van de voornoemde Pro-vintie en Rechtbanken / &c. aldaar.

Waar by noch gevoeght is een Beſchrijving van de Hooft-Stadt
PHILADELPHIA.

Nu onlangs uytgeſet, en gelegen tuſchen twee Navigable Rivieren, namentlijk : tuſchen *Delaware* en *Schuylkil.*

Ende een verhaal van de voorſpoedige en voordeelige ſtandt van ſaken van de voornoemde Societeyt binnen de voornoemde Stadt en Provintie / &c. Waar by noch komt een Voor-reden / gevende een korte onderrechtinge van de Conditien / hoe de Gouverneur ſijn Landt nu verkoopt / en verhuurt op een eeuwige Erf-pacht / als mede van eenige van de voornaamſte Wetten / &c.

Den tweeden Druk.

t'AMSTERDAM,
By JACOB CLAUS, Boekverkooper in de Prince-ſtraat, 1684.

Title Page of a Dutch Translation of One of William Penn's
Early Promotional Tracts

contribute from its own strength to the growing strength of Pennsylvania. But the migration from Britain also continued until by 1700, it has been estimated, there may have been as many Quakers in the colonies as in all the British Isles together. These were by no means all recent immigrants, for Quakerism still had much of its original evangelical zeal, and converts lived in many different parts of the colonies. But the Delaware Valley had become the great seat of Quaker settlement in America, and as that settlement grew, West Jersey grew, though much more slowly than did Pennsylvania. It has been estimated that at the opening of the eighteenth century West Jersey had approximately thirty-five hundred people, among them perhaps four hundred Swedes and Finns who, for the most part, represented a migration across the river during the preceding quarter-century. There were also a few recent immigrants from New England and a scattering of others, but the population remained, as it would for many years thereafter, one made up predominantly of Quakers of English and Irish origins.

By 1700 the estimated population of Pennsylvania had reached a total of almost eighteen-thousand persons.* This was substantially larger even than the estimated total for all New Jersey of just over fourteen thousand. Since West Jersey

* This figure does not include the additional twenty-five hundred people living below Pennsylvania proper in the area which later formed the state of Delaware, but which at this time was under the government of Pennsylvania.

An Historical and Geographical Account

OF THE

PROVINCE and COUNTRY

OF

PENSILVANIA;

AND OF

West-New-Jersey

IN

AMERICA.

The Richness of the Soil, the Sweetness of the Situation, the Wholesomness of the Air, the Navigable Rivers, and others, the prodigious Encrease of Corn, the flourishing Condition of the City of *Philadelphia*, with the stately Buildings, and other Improvements there. The strange Creatures, as *Birds*, *Beasts*, *Fishes*, and *Fowls*, with the several sorts of *Minerals*, *Purging Waters*, and *Stones*, lately discovered. The *Natives*, *Aborigines*, their Language, *Religion*, *Laws*, and *Customs*; The first Planters, the *Dutch*, *Sweeds*, and *English*, with the number of its Inhabitants; As also a Touch upon *George Keith's New Religion*, in his second Change since he left the *QUAKERS.*

With a Map of both Countries.

By GABRIEL THOMAS,
who resided there about Fifteen Years.

London, Printed for, and Sold by *A. Baldwin*, at the *Oxon Arms* in *Warwick-Lane*, 1698.

Title Page of an Account by Gabriel Thomas Published in
London in 1698

certainly could claim no more than four thousand, it will be seen that East Jersey, with a probable population now of over ten thousand, had grown much more impressively than had the Quaker part of the province. If West Jersey be grouped with Pennsylvania, however, the total for the Quaker settlements of the Delaware Valley reaches a figure somewhere between twenty-one and twenty-two thousand people.* For a migration of comparably impressive proportions it is necessary to turn back to the great Puritan migration into New England during the 1630's.

* The figures used here are from *Historical Statistics of the United States, Colonial Times to 1957* (Bureau of the Census: Washington, 1960), 756.

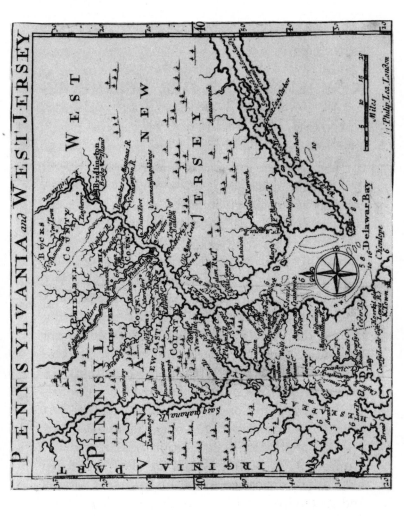

From Gabriel Thomas, *An Historical and Geographical Account of the Province and Country of Pennsilvania; and of West-New-Jersey in America*, London, 1698

revenues, which depended heavily upon excise duties, had suffered in consequence, and at a time when quit-rents offered no substantial supplement to income. East Jersey was the most rapidly growing agricultural community in the neighborhood of New York City, but that area belonged to a separate jurisdiction which entertained its own ambitions for the development of competitive ports at Newark, Elizabeth, and especially Perth Amboy, the capital city founded by Scottish settlers at the mouth of the Raritan in 1683. In this competition New York enjoyed the advantage, in part no doubt because of the value of her export of furs. Long since the fur trade had passed beyond the stage at which any colonist might trade profitably with his immediate Indian neighbors to one in which the profit depended upon an opportunity to exploit more distant sources of the beaver skins which commanded the best prices in Europe. In this development, New York, or more exactly, Albany held a distinct advantage, largely because of the arrangements its traders had managed to make with the strategically situated Iroquois. Nevertheless, New York's governors found repeated cause to complain of a continuing loss to provincial revenues resulting from New Jersey's attempt to pursue its own independent course. They complained also that New Jersey imposed a constant drain upon New York's limited population, with a resulting loss not only of manpower but also of quit-rents.

Although considerations of space forbid exploration of the problem, there is no reason for doubting the special difficulties confronting New York's government after 1665. In addition to factors mentioned above, there were heavy military costs to be met during a period which witnessed two wars with Holland and the opening rounds of the great contest with France for supremacy on the North American continent. Whether the foe be Dutch or French, New York's strategic location demanded costly military expenditures.

In the opinion of all the early governors of New York, the repossession of New Jersey was a necessary step toward solving the problem. Two attempts to accomplish that end were actually made, both of them by Sir Edmund Andros: the first, soon after the close of the third Anglo-Dutch war in 1674, and the second in 1688, just on the eve of a long series of wars with France.

When Andros reached New York late in 1674 for the purpose of taking over the province from the Dutch, he carried a commission making him governor of the entire area covered by the Duke of York's extraordinary charter. Being a soldier, like Richard Nicolls, Governor Andros promptly showed an inclination to follow his instructions to the letter, much to the disturbance of both the Connecticut and the New Jersey jurisdictions. In this effort he soon met frustration because of the contradictory actions of his superior. Nevertheless, he persisted thereafter in a running quarrel with East Jersey's government, especially over its right to establish free ports in competition with New York City. Andros even placed Governor Philip Carteret under arrest in 1680 and carried him to New York for trial, where a jury refused to convict. For this action Andros, of course, has been severely criticized, but surely the ultimate blame belongs to the Duke of York. It is pertinent to note that Carteret's arrest and trial came after Governor Andros had visited England in 1678. While there he was knighted, and presumably he also received some clarification of his instructions, or at least thought he did. Before 1680 had passed Sir Edmund was called home to answer charges regarding his administration of New York's revenues. Of these charges in due course he was cleared. And eight years after his recall, Andros was back, this time as governor-general of the Dominion of New England, to proclaim the incorporation of both New York and New Jersey into a jurisdiction even more sweeping in its geographical extent than had been the original claims of the Duke of York.

This extraordinary administrative experiment, which might have changed the whole course of American history, is probably less attributable to deliberate design than to an unusual combination of circumstances. One of these was the accession of the New York proprietor to the throne in 1685 as James II. New York thus automatically became a royal colony, with the immediate result that its affairs for the first time fell directly under the supervision of the king's chief advisers on colonial questions, who were the members of a standing committee of the Privy Council commonly known as the Lords of Trade. After its establishment in 1675, the committee had become involved in a long struggle with Massachusetts, partly because of its general interest in a more effective enforcement of the Navigation Acts but even more, one suspects, simply because of a desire to bring the recalcitrant Puritan leaders of that province into a proper submission to their king. A final victory had come as recently as 1684, by way of a court decree annulling the Massachusetts charter. An interim government of the colony was established under Joseph Dudley, a native of the province, while the Lords of Trade considered what permanent disposition of the question might be made. For some time past the committee had shown an inclination to look critically upon any colonial charter which interposed a special authority, either corporate or proprietary, between the colonists and the king. For example, the Lords of Trade had opposed the grant of Pennsylvania to William Penn. Their subsequent victory over Massachusetts naturally encouraged them to consider the possibility that other charters might be annulled. In short, they were in a receptive mood for complaints against any and all colonial charters.

Among those who were quick to enter such

complaints was Governor Thomas Dongan of New York, successor in that office to Sir Edmund Andros. Although he had avoided Sir Edmund's aggressiveness in dealing with East Jersey, he was nonetheless perplexed as to how the defenses of New York, and especially of Albany, could be financed in the face of an impending contest with the French in Canada. While doing what he could to strengthen the colony's defenses, he complained to London of inadequate revenues and of the way in which the people of New York were "cooped up" at the very center of the king's dominions in North America.* His complaints thus provided further encouragement to an investigation of the possibility that effective action might be taken against the jurisdictions, among others, of New Jersey, Connecticut, and Rhode Island.

When it was decided to send Sir Edmund Andros as royal governor to Boston in 1686, it is doubtful that either the king or his advisors had anything more in mind than the unification of the New England colonies, whose own earlier confederation had provided a suggestive precedent. It may be significant, however, that the man chosen for the job was a soldier who had served as the governor of New York, and who for that reason could be expected to have a helpfully broad view of the strategic considerations affecting the defenses of the English colonies. It certainly

---

* Quoted in Charles M. Andrews, *The Colonial Period of American History* (4 vols.; New Haven, 1934-1938), III, 120.

is significant that in the enforced submission of Connecticut and Rhode Island to the Dominion government, their peoples were given cause to assume that they had only a choice between submitting to the Boston government or being incorporated into another union to be governed from New York. That any plan for such a second union actually existed, even in a tentative form, is doubtful. It perhaps was enough that Long Island long since had been taken by New York, that Andros himself was well remembered for earlier attempts to extend New York's jurisdiction to the Connecticut and to the Delaware, and that Governor Dongan had been pressing on London the peculiar needs of his "cooped up" people. The solution of New York's problem that was actually attempted was its annexation, together with New Jersey, to the Dominion of New England.

Having brought all of New England into submission, Sir Edmund journeyed to New York for the purpose of proclaiming its annexation in the summer of 1688. He then crossed the Hudson to proclaim the annexation of East Jersey at Elizabeth on August 11, and of West Jersey at Burlington on August 18. From the coasts of Maine to the Delaware River there then existed only one recognized jurisdiction, for the scheme was not that of a federal union, or anything like it. Former provincial distinctions were to be obliterated and the people of the several provinces brought directly under a single unitary authority. But the further details need not detain us here.

The Dominion of New England had a very short life. Within a few weeks after Andros visited New Jersey the government of James II was overthrown in a bloodless revolution Englishmen remember as the Glorious Revolution. William of Orange, a Dutch prince, and his wife Mary, Protestant daughter of the Catholic James II, were brought jointly to the throne. The news of these developments at home, reaching America in 1689, led to another bloodless revolution in Boston which, for all practical purposes, marked the end of the Dominion of New England. As Rhode Island and Connecticut reinstated their former governments under the charters they had received from Charles II, and Jacob Leisler took charge in New York, where Andros had left a lieutenant-governor for his assistance in administering the more westerly parts of the Dominion, the disintegration of that jurisdiction became complete.

Although New Jersey experienced no revolutionary disturbance of the sort that followed in New York with Leisler's so-called rebellion, the collapse of the Dominion left her in a difficult situation. For three years thereafter no one knew, quite literally, who had the power of government in New Jersey. The annexation to the Dominion of New England had seemed to mark a final repudiation of the previously challenged right of the proprietors to govern, but the Revolution in

England had re-opened the question and the government there was slow to decide. King William headed a revolutionary regime confronted with many difficult issues of domestic politics. He headed also a diplomatic and military alliance which was at war with Louis XIV of France, and in Ireland the new king faced a rebellion in behalf of James II. It took a while to get around to the problems of New Jersey. The Lords of Trade favored its annexation to New York, but the influence of that committee was in decline and not until 1696, when the Board of Trade was established, would there be an agency of the English government capable of exerting the influence on policy formerly held by the Lords of Trade. When Benjamin Fletcher was commissioned in 1692 as Governor of New York and Pennsylvania, where William Penn's right of government had been suspended, partly because of his former friendship with James II, the original draft of the commission also included New Jersey. But the proprietors succeeded in having New Jersey struck from the commission on the assurance that their colony would cooperate in the defense of Albany. They were then permitted to reassert their own authority by issuing separate commissions to Andrew Hamilton, formerly deputy-governor in East Jersey, to serve as governor both of East and West Jersey.

This victory of the proprietors, however, was destined to be short lived. After 1696, the newly established Board of Trade showed a hostility toward the colonial charters that was comparable to that formerly displayed by the Lords of Trade. The Board made no attempt to revive the Dominion of New England. Nor did it try anything like it, except for the encouragement it gave to continuing experiment with the idea that colonies having the same man for governor might the better cooperate for military purposes. This hope, generally doomed to disappointment, undoubtedly influenced the Board in setting its main goal, which was to bring all of the colonies under the direct rule of the king. The Board of Trade's efforts to achieve that goal, vigorously pursued for several years, included more than one attempt to secure enactment of a comprehensive statute by Parliament. But in the end, the Board had to be content with a single victory—the negotiated surrender to the king in 1702 of the rights to government in New Jersey.

The New Jersey proprietors were peculiarly vulnerable. From the very beginning their claim to jurisdictional rights had rested upon an uncertain legal foundation. Moreover, the repeated challenges to that claim had kept the question to the fore, and linked it with the most serious issues of imperial administration and security. Worse still, perhaps, was the fact that the New Jersey proprietorship in its extraordinary development had become a virtually indefensible absurdity, if compared with any reasonable standard of colonial administration. Another volume in this series is devoted to the complex history of the proprietors, and the discussion here can be brief. It is almost enough merely to observe that before the close of the century there were at least twenty-four proprietors of East Jersey, and an almost indeterminable number of proprietors for West Jersey. As previously has been noted, Sir George Carteret's rights to East Jersey had been purchased in 1682 by twelve men, mostly Quakers. These twelve soon had taken in others, until the number was doubled. In the case of West Jersey, Edward Byllynge's rights had been sold, after his death in 1685, to Dr. Daniel Coxe, a colorful adventurer in schemes of American settlement for many years thereafter. Having made the purchase in 1687, just before New Jersey's inclusion in the Dominion of New England, Coxe became discouraged enough over the prospects in West Jersey to sell his rights in 1692. This sale placed the nominal rights of government in the hands of the 48 members of the West Jersey Society. There was some overlapping in the membership of the two groups of proprietors. Some of them had residence in New Jersey, others were absentee landlords with little interest in the province beyond the returns they hoped to get on their investment. Their collective judgment in the choice of agents was not always perfect, and there were factional disturbances in the colony. To cut the story short—it will be discussed elsewhere in the Series, more fully and with more regard for technical complexity—this was no way to run a colony.

Finally, a deal was negotiated with the Board of Trade by which the proprietors retained full title to the soil in return for a surrender of their "pretended" rights of government. The New Jersey proprietorship thus survived, as indeed anachronistically it does to the present day, but the government of the province after 1702 was the King's.

Among the proposals submitted to the Board of Trade during the negotiations, one would have eliminated New Jersey altogether as a separate province. Edward Randolph, surveyor-general of the customs and former secretary to the Dominion of New England, suggested in 1701 that East Jersey be annexed to New York and West Jersey to Pennsylvania. This suggestion might have received more serious attention than it apparently did had the Board of Trade been more successful in its general campaign against the colonial charters, including that of William Penn. Instead, it was decided in 1702 to unite East and West Jersey under a single government, with representation divided equally between the two in an assembly that would meet alternately at Perth Amboy and at Burlington. But significantly the choice for the first royal governor fell to Lord Cornbury, recently commissioned Governor of New York. The governor of New York continued to double as the governor of New Jersey until 1738, when for the first time New Jersey got a governor of its

Courtesy of the Princeton University Library

own. With its chief executive normally resident in New York City, the province of New Jersey had in effect three capital cities: Perth Amboy, Burlington, and New York.

The governor was to rule in New Jersey with the aid of an appointed council of twelve men and an assembly initially composed of 24 elected members. For exercise of the franchise the possession of one hundred acres of land was required. To qualify for membership in the assembly the requirement was one thousand acres. This was hardly so popular a body as had been envisioned in the Burlington Concessions and Agreements of 1677. Nor were the assembly's powers quite so great as those originally conceded to it by Berkeley and Carteret in the Concessions and Agreement of 1665. It should not be assumed, however, that the introduction of royal government brought as radical a departure from previous practice as at first glance it might appear. Circumstances, and disagreements between the people and the proprietors, had long prevented full implementation of either of these famous documents. Their importance lies not so much in the letter of their original provisions as in the solid foundation they provided for a continuing belief that government was limited in its lawful exercise of power by the rights belonging to the people. The requirement that a man have one hundred acres of land to exercise the franchise brought New Jersey into line with the general trend in colonial America toward identification of the franchise with a freehold title to property. It was a requirement that was not too difficult to meet in eighteenth-century New Jersey, for the colony had become a land, in the main, of modest but independent farmers.

At the local level of government, the transition to royal rule brought little change. East Jersey had been divided into the original counties of Bergen, Essex, Middlesex, and Monmouth as early as 1683. The division had come a little later in West Jersey, where by 1692 four counties had been established: Burlington, Gloucester, Salem, and Cape May. Once more, one finds occasion to emphasize the parallel between developments in New Jersey and in neighboring provinces. Richard Nicolls had set a pattern for local administration throughout the middle colonies by the establishment of Kings County and by the appointment of resident magistrates in other parts of what had been New Netherland. The jurisdictions presided over by three courts on the west bank of the Delaware had often been described as counties before William Penn took possession of the area and acquired his own colony of Pennsylvania. Finding a familiar and functioning model of local administration ready at hand, he divided Pennsylvania into three counties and gave them courts very similar to those found downriver. The formal division of New York into counties came, as in

East Jersey, in 1683. New Jersey differed from her neighbors chiefly in the number of offices in the county which were filled by election.

The influence of royal government in New Jersey was by no means limited to the political sphere. Since the royal governor was usually a communicant of the established Church of England, he naturally sought to advance its interest in the province. If he showed hesitancy in doing so, he was prompted to stir himself by London, where the influential Society for the Propagation of the Gospel in Foreign Parts had been organized in 1701 as the agency of a newly-awakened missionary zeal in the Anglican Church. New Jersey, with a population virtually half Puritan in its origins and half Quaker, naturally became an object of the society's attention. Missionaries were sent, and the governor even sponsored abortive legislation for the establishment of the church in New Jersey. The Anglicans made progress in the eighteenth century, but the colony as a whole remained true to its origins as a community of religious dissenters. Indeed, the most rapidly growing new denomination at this time was that of the Presbyterians. Depending for their growth partly upon the migration of new settlers from northern Ireland and Scotland and partly upon the zeal and eloquence of their clergymen during the Great Awakening, a religious revival sweeping through the colonies in the 1730's and 1740's, the Presbyterians greatly reinforced the influence of Calvinistic principles and standards of conduct in the colony. If a plurality of religious belief, and refusal to accept the authority of any one church on grounds other than those dictated by the individual conscience, can be described as distinctively American, New Jersey was among the first of the English colonies to become American.

Her people also held true to an earlier prejudice against landlords. Although more than one decision had been lost to the proprietors on the issue of quit-rents, the New Jersey farmer paid his rents grudgingly, when he paid them at all. New immigrants often became squatters, refusing even to take out titles from the proprietors, and the colony was disturbed by more than one rent riot. More important than the attitude of the squatters was the sympathetic support they often received from the older inhabitants. The Jerseyman who wrote the following lines to the *New York Weekly Post-Boy* in 1746 spoke for many others, some long dead, when he declared:

No man is naturally entitled to a greater proportion of the earth than another; but tho' it was made for the use of all, it may nevertheless be appropriated by every individual. This is done by the improvement of any part of it lying vacant, which is thereby distinguished from the great common of nature, and made the property of that man who bestowed his labor on it, from whom it cannot afterwards be taken without breaking thro' the rules of Natural Justice; for thereby he could be actually deprived of the Fruits of his Industry.*

The fact that this statement of principle was borrowed from John Locke robs it of no part of its significance as a statement of conviction born also of the long experience of New Jersey's settlers.

The argument is worth a second glance, for it tells us much about the background of the American Revolution. Deeply rooted in the experience of all the colonists, the propositions advanced by this Jerseyman point unmistakably to basic assumptions that helped to unite the colonies in their resistance to a new attempt, this time under the leadership of Parliament, to strengthen the authority of the imperial government. The ultimate revolt of the colonists has no single, or simple, explanation, but there can be no doubt that during the long debate which preceded the Revolution Americans came to view the issue as one involving a central question of who it was who had the best title to America. To them, of course, the answer was obvious, for had not they, and their fathers, very largely on their own initiative and at their own cost, taken up vacant land and by their labors made it into a goodly in-

* Quoted in Lawrence H. Gipson, *The British Empire Before the American Revolution:* Vol. III, *The Northern Plantations* (Caldwell, Idaho, 1936), 152-153.

heritance? Could they rightfully be deprived of the fruits of their own industry?

Perhaps it was because so much of the fighting, and the maneuvering of armies during the War, took place on New Jersey's fertile acres that she became the third of the states to ratify the Federal Constitution when the fighting was done. Perhaps it was because her inhabitants remembered the continuing problem in late colonial years of being a neighbor to New York and Pennsylvania. Only on the eve of the Revolution had a frequently turbulent dispute with New York over the colony's northern boundary found a final settlement. No comparably bitter quarrel had marred New Jersey's relations with Pennsylvania, but Philadelphia, like New York City, still held a long lead over the competing ports of New Jersey. Having won in the Constitutional Convention a compromise intended to protect the smaller and less advantageously situated states, New Jersey unhesitatingly cast her lot with the new Union.

It was altogether consistent with her history that she should have done so. Placed geographically at the very center of the middle colonies and states, New Jersey had ever been denied full freedom to pursue an independent existence, and the extent of her dependence upon neighboring communities measured too their dependence upon her. If we look, for example, to the cultural development of the colony, it is necessary to observe that New Jersey was among the last of the English colonies in North America to acquire a printing press of its own, and very much for the same reason that many of its citizens today read a New York or Philadelphia newspaper in preference to one published within the State. But New Jersey was also the only one of these colonies which on the eve of the Revolution could boast of two educational institutions of collegiate rank—Princeton and Rutgers, as we know them today—and each of them served a larger community than the one in which it was located.

BIBLIOGRAPHICAL NOTE

Because another volume in the Tercentenary Series contains a discussion of the bibliography for New Jersey's colonial history, it will be enough here to observe that the latest and most authoritative accounts of the colony's first years are found in two studies by John E. Pomfret, *The Province of West New Jersey, 1609-1702* (Princeton, 1956), and *The Province of East New Jersey, 1609-1702* (Princeton, 1962).

For the larger subject of English colonization in North America during the seventeenth century, the bibliography is both extensive and complex. Only a few of the more important, or especially helpful, works can be mentioned here.

Charles M. Andrews, *The Colonial Period of American History* (4 vols., New Haven, 1934-1938) is the standard authority in the field. The first three volumes provide a connected narrative for the entire period of the original settlements. No more authoritative account of the movement of settlement in the second half of the century can be found than that contained in Professor Andrews' third volume, which is devoted to New York, New Jersey, Pennsylvania, and the two Carolinas. The final volume deals broadly, and very nearly definitively, with the origins and development of *England's Commercial and Colonial Policy*. Andrews' suggestive essays on *The Colonial Background of the American Revolution* (New Haven, 1924; reprinted in paperback, 1961) are strongly recommended for those who wish to read a less detailed study providing an overall view of the colonial period. For a comprehensive interpretation of the earlier phase of England's colonial expansion in North America, still another short study by the same author can be recommended: *Our Earliest Colonial Settlements* (New York, 1933; reprinted in paperback, Ithaca, 1959).

Wesley Frank Craven, *The Southern Colonies in the Seventeenth Century, 1607-1689* (Baton Rouge, 1949) is the standard account for that area. Among earlier studies of a comprehensive character, Herbert L. Osgood, *The American Colonies in the Seventeenth Century* (3 vols.; New York, 1904; reprinted by Peter Smith, Gloucester, Mass., 1957) remains useful, especially for its treatment of institutional history. Wallace Notestein's much more recent *The English People on the Eve of Colonization, 1603-1630* (New York, 1954) is a very readable account of English society and institutions written by an eminent authority for Americans who are interested in the English background of their own history. The book is one of the volumes in the "New American Nation Series," now in process of publication by Harper &

Brothers, who recently (1962) have made it available in a paperback edition. In the same series, and also in paperback, will be found Louis B. Wright's informative study of *The Cultural Life of the American Colonies, 1607-1763* (New York, 1957). Thomas Jefferson Wertenbaker, *The Founding of American Civilization: the Middle Colonies* (New York, 1938) is an engagaing social history and one of the very few studies which deals comprehensively with the Middle Colonies.

Among the many significant works published in recent years on the subject of the New England Puritans, perhaps Edmund S. Morgan, *The Puritan Dilemma: the Story of John Winthrop* (Boston, 1958; reprinted in paperback, 1963) is the first to be recommended for the general reader. Perry Miller's *Orthodoxy in Massachusetts, 1630-1650* (Cambridge, 1933) is a seminal study. Miller's *Roger Williams': His Contribution to the American Tradition* (Indianapolis, 1953; reprinted in paperback, New York, 1962) offers sure guidance on a difficult and often misunderstood topic. Professor Miller's *The New England Mind: the Seventeenth Century* (Cambridge, 1939) and *The New England Mind: from Colony to Province* (Cambridge, 1953) are both written for the mature student. A sensitive and suggestive narrative is found in Ola Elizabeth Winslow, *Meetinghouse Hill, 1630-1783* (New York, 1952).

Bernard Bailyn, *The New England Merchants in the Seventeenth Century* (Cambridge, 1955) is an especially valuable study of economics, society, and politics. Isabel M. Calder, *The New Haven Colony* (New Haven, 1934) is the authority on a subject of great importance for New Jersey's history. Dixon Ryan Fox, *Yankees and Yorkers* (New York, 1940) traces, with skill and humor, the long conflict between the New England Puritans and their Dutch and English neighbors on the Hudson. Richard S. Dunn, *Puritans and Yankees: the Winthrop Dynasty of New England, 1630-1717* Princeton, 1962) is especially valuable for the light it throws upon John Winthrop, Jr. and his enterprizes. Viola F. Barnes, *The Dominion of New England* (New Haven, 1923) remains the standard account of that extraordinary administrative experiment.

New York's early history, so closely intertwined with that of New Jersey, is a sadly neglected subject. The most informative overall account is that of John R. Brodhead, *The History of the State of New York, 1609-1691* (2 vols.; New York, 1853-1871) but, in addition to being long out of print, it is unreadable. Many of the myths that have grown up around the figure of Peter Stuyvesant are cheerfully dismissed by Henry H. Kessler and Eugene Rachlis in their *Peter Stuyvesant and His New York* (New York, 1959), a good piece of historical writing. Much less readable, but extremely valuable for the damage it does to the mythology of the New York patroons is S. G. Nissenson, *The Patroon's Domain* (New York, 1937). Very helpful, too, is Lawrence H. Leder, *Robert Livingston, 1654-1728, and the Politics of Colonial New York* (Chapel Hill, 1961). It is to be hoped that these more recent studies bring with them the promise of further study in this area, for there is good reason for believing that New York's story holds the key to many other significant chapters in our colonial history.

Amandus Johnson, *Swedish Settlements on the Delaware, 1638-1644* (2 vols.; Philadelphia, 1911) is definitive and of much less interest to students of New Jersey's history than often is assumed, for the Swedes came late to the Jersey side of the river.

The literature of Quakerism approaches in volume that of Puritanism. Frederick B. Tolles, *Meeting House and Counting House: the Quaker Merchants of Colonial Philadelphia, 1682-1763* (Chapel Hill, 1948) provides for the general student an especially helpful introduction to an understanding of the Quakers' place in our history. His *Quakers and the Atlantic Culture* (New York, 1960), particularly the first two chapters, should also be read. Rufus M. Jones, *The Quakers in the American Colonies* (London, 1911) is a classic among the earlier studies. Pomfret's summary account in his *West Jersey*, previously cited, is an important contribution to our knowledge of Quaker settlement in America. Among the several biographies of Penn, the latest and perhaps the best is Catherine Owens Peare, *William Penn* (Philadelphia, 1957). Edwin B. Bronner, *William*

Penn's "Holy Experiment": the Founding of Pennsylvania, 1681-1701 (New York, 1962) provides a useful and somewhat conventional summary of the colony's first years.

A final word may be in order. As more than one item in the foregoing list will have suggested, it is possible now to own at low cost a reasonably full library in early American history simply by buying paperback editions.

INDEX

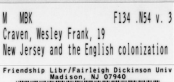

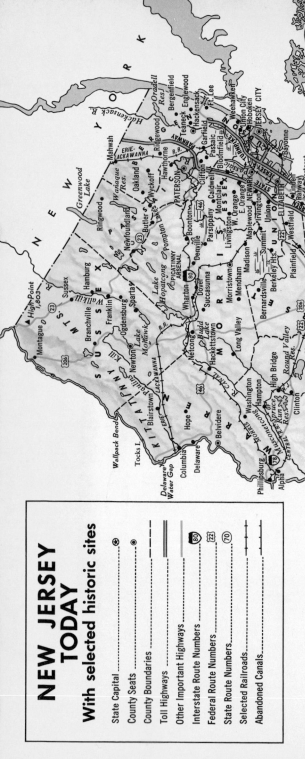

NEW JERSEY TODAY
With selected historic sites

State Capital	⊛
County Seats	⊙
County Boundaries	
Toll Highways	
Other Important Highways	
Interstate Route Numbers	80
Federal Route Numbers	221
State Route Numbers	70
Selected Railroads	
Abandoned Canals	

SCALE OF MILES

0 10 20 30 40 50